THE NATURE AND NECESSITY

OF INTEREST

THE NATURE AND NECESSITY OF INTEREST

BY

GUSTAV CASSEL

[1903]

REPRINTS OF ECONOMIC CLASSICS

AUGUSTUS M. KELLEY · PUBLISHERS

NEW YORK 1971

First Edition 1903

(New York: The Macmillan Company, 1903)

REPRINTED 1956, 1971 BY

AUGUSTUS M. KELLEY · PUBLISHERS

REPRINTS OF ECONOMIC CLASSICS

New York New York 10001

. . . .

I S B N 0-678-00848-5

L C N 77-147898

. . . .

PRINTED IN THE UNITED STATES OF AMERICA

by SENTRY PRESS, NEW YORK, N. Y. 10019

PREFACE

THERE are some scientific problems such, *e.g.*, as the "Squaring of the Circle" in mathematics, which seem to have engaged the attention of humanity since the very earliest stages of civilisation, but of which the definite solution has been reserved for the efforts of the present age.

The problem of Interest belongs to this class. Indeed we find it dealt with as early as modern historical research is able to go back ; and it reflects at every step of its development the attainments and the aims of contemporary life. Economic investigations of the last two or three centuries have thrown light upon almost every side of the problem ; and, to construct a theory, there hardly remains more than to present, as a consistent and systematic whole, what is already known as a multitude of scattered observations. It is incumbent upon the present generation to bring about this final solution of a problem which has claimed so large a part of the efforts of previous ages.

We devote considerable energy to the discovery of the North Pole or to the exploration of the deserts of Asia. We do not do this for any immediate practical benefit, but simply because we

cannot rid ourselves of the feeling that we are
bound to know the globe on which it is our lot to
dwell. Is it not, then, even more urgent that we
should comprehend the nature of Interest, and
enable ourselves to trace the causes and effects of a
phenomenon so intimately connected with our every-
day life?

The problem of interest presents, however, not
only and not even primarily, this historical or
philosophical aspect. It is most emphatically a
practical problem. In its earlier stages the discussion of interest turns essentially on what we now
call usury. Though this side of the problem has
lost its previous pre-eminence, it still remains an
important subject for practical politics, and we
cannot hope to deal with it profitably without
thoroughly knowing the nature of the evil and the
end we wish to attain. In our days the problem of
interest has, to a great extent, changed its nature
and has become principally a problem of social distribution. Looked at from this point of view,
interest can of course be studied only as an integral
part of the problem of Distribution, which is again,
as we shall see, only a side of a problem to which
we shall have to pay special attention, the general
problem of Prices.

It also follows from this modern view of the
problem of interest, that we can never hope to get a
really good grasp of what is called the Social
Question, without having thoroughly penetrated
into the nature of interest. The Socialist School of
the 19th century has largely identified the Labour

Cause with the abolition of interest ; and the whole modern discussion of the Social Question has, mainly in consequence of this error, become so interwoven with allusions to the effects of interest and the right or wrong of it, that we cannot, at the present moment, enter on any investigation of the wages question without stumbling at almost every step on the problem of interest. This shows, perhaps better than anything else, the eminently practical value of a right theory of interest.

To write such a theory has seemed to me of such paramount importance that I have felt justified in devoting to the task the greater part of the last six years. The final issue of these efforts is given in the present volume. Some preliminary results have been published already ; and for the more intricate questions of the theory, the reader is referred to these publications. The work that has to be gone through, in order to get to the bottom of the interest question, is not always of the very lightest kind ; but I have endeavoured to make the present exposition of the matter as simple as possible, and I have not included in the text anything that might prove an obstacle to the ordinary reader.

I have devoted the first chapter to a survey of the historical development of the theory of interest. In this I have not tried to give anything like a complete history of the problem, my main purpose being to state the results hitherto obtained, and in this way to make the present investigation profit by the efforts of three centuries.

The positive theory of interest is preceded by a

chapter on the general theory of prices, with a view particularly to show what is the purpose and the use of prices, and thus establish their social necessity. For some of the more difficult points of this theory, the reader is referred to three papers that I have published in the "Zeitschrift für die gesamte Staatswissenschaft" during the last three years.

This foundation being laid, interest can be treated as a price determined by the demand for, and the supply of, a certain service. The causes governing the demand and the supply of that service, are examined in the two following chapters, and these contain, in fact, the central part of the theory of interest. The relations of interest to money are shortly discussed in the fifth chapter. It is particularly necessary to touch upon this side of the problem, because the general theory of prices has been built upon the assumption that a money scale can be taken for granted.

The necessity of interest having been established, so far as the present form of social organisation is concerned, by the investigations of the third and fourth chapters, I proceed in the sixth chapter to prove that interest would have to be paid even in a Socialist Community. Hence it follows that interest is an absolute element of economic life. This chapter is a short summary of my book " Das Recht auf den vollen Arbeitsertrag " (Göttingen, 1900).

In the final chapter, I endeavour to show that an accurate theory of interest is not merely the concern of a handful of scientific economists, but a matter of great practical importance. For it gives us a clear and adequate conception of the old problem of usury as well as of the more modern and more general problem of social distribution, and therefore it takes us far on the road towards the solution of these weighty problems.

I have to express my grateful acknowledgments to the many friends who have corrected the English text or otherwise assisted me in preparing this volume for the press. Professor Smart has read the MS. as well as all the proofs, and I feel very much indebted to him for many useful suggestions and criticisms.

This book is published with a subvention from the Swedish Government's " Fund for the Publication of Scientific Works."

G. C.

DJURSHOLM, STOCKHOLM, SWEDEN.
    July, 1903.

CONTENTS

CHAPTER I

OUTLINES OF THE HISTORICAL DEVELOPMENT OF THE THEORY OF INTEREST

CHAPTER II

ON PRICES IN GENERAL AND ON INTEREST CONSIDERED AS A PRICE

CHAPTER III

DEMAND FOR WAITING

CONTENTS

THE NATURE AND NECESSITY OF INTEREST

CHAPTER I

OUTLINES OF THE HISTORICAL DEVELOPMENT OF THE THEORY OF INTEREST

§ 1. *The Canonist view of interest*

CRITICISM cannot be very fruitful unless the critic really tries to come to a deeper understanding of the views of those whom he means to criticise, and unless he starts from the assumption that they have had *some* reason for their opinions. This is true even with regard to the Canonist view of interest. Certainly, the rigid suppression of interest by the mediæval Church must at first sight seem very strange to a modern mind: we naturally feel inclined to look upon this prohibition as an outcome of mere narrowness and folly. But more careful investigations show that there are very plausible explanations and even some sensible grounds for the mediæval policy against interest. Historical writers tell us that, in those times, the great majority of all loans were made for unproductive purposes, and thus had the character of a temporary assistance to persons in bad economic conditions. *Bentham* has pointed out how, under such circumstances, the borrower is generally an object of popular sympathy, the lender not.[1] This general sympathy gains not only in strength, but even very materially in reason, if, as so often was the case in mediæval times, the lender is a rich man in a somewhat monopolistic position, oppressing the poor and ignorant borrower by gradually depriving him of the very means of gaining his livelihood.[2] Thus, as *Ashley* remarks, "the Church, caring for the masses of the people, for the weak and the stupid, might think it well to maintain a prohibition which imposed no restriction on the activity of the traders in the towns, who were well enough able to take care of themselves. The original prohibition had really aimed at preventing the oppression of the weak by the economically strong.[3] One might ask nowadays if it would not, for this purpose, have been a better policy to have regulated interest and prohibited an excessive rate, than to have altogether prohibited any loans, except those few which might be granted gratuitously. We must, however, remember that interest in general could be at that time condemned as a sin against the Law of God ; while interest above the rate of 6 or 10 per cent. could not be. Thus we may not find it quite unreasonable that the Church, compelled to choose between prohibiting interest on the one hand, and giving up every restriction on transactions in loans

[1] "Those who have the resolution to sacrifice the present to the future, are natural objects of envy to those who have sacrificed the future to the present. The children who have eaten their cake are the natural enemies of the children who have theirs." "It is the general interest of those with whom a man lives, that his expenses should be at least as great as his circumstances will bear." *Defence of Usury*, London 1787 ; Letter X.

[2] "By far the greater part of the population of western Europe continued to be engaged in the old unchanging pursuits of agriculture : a declaration that payment could be taken for the loan of money would have meant the delivering them into the hands of the spoiler." *Ashley, W. J.*, An Introduction to English Economic History and Theory. London 1893, Part II. Ch. VI.

[3] Ibid.

on the other, regarded the former alternative as the
only possible one ; and we may perhaps even admit
that the policy of the Church, under the given
circumstances, added more to "the sum total of
human happiness" than it took from it.[1]

Many a severe critic of the Church, from the time
of *Bentham* to that of *Lecky*,[2] has probably overlooked, or at least undervalued, the rational grounds
for the interest policy of the Canonists.   But we
must not, therefore, push our rehabilitation of the
Canonists too far.   Even if we admit that there was
some practical advantage in their policy, it is impossible not to recognise in what an exceedingly bad
position the *theory* of interest was thereby placed.
The Canonists defended their case by two methods
which have always proved fatal to the development
of strong and clear reasoning, viz., by *Sophistry*,
the worst degeneration of human thought, and by
Appeal to Authority, the suppression of thought.

The necessity of carrying on business with
borrowed money became more and more frequent
and urgent as trade developed during the latter part
of the Middle Ages.   Thus the Canonists saw themselves forced, not only to tolerate many forms for the
payment of money-advances, but also to invent
distinctions between those forms and the "*usura*,"
the payment for the mere use of money.   For this
purpose it was that the whole arsenal of sophistical
argument was brought into action.   What was by
nature *one* thing was, by artificial distinctions, split
up into many.   And thus were created conditions
extremely unfavourable for scientific investigations
into the nature of interest.[3]

[1] Comp. *Marshall*, Principles of Economics, Vol. I., 4th Ed.
Book VI. Ch. VI. § 2.
[2] Comp. *Lecky*, History of the Rise and Influence of the
Spirit of Rationalism in Europe, 1865.
[3] We might accept *Ashley's* opinion that it never was the aim

The most important cases where payment for a loan could be claimed,[1] were the discounting of bills and the lending of money to a business man under the form of partnership in his business. To these were added two other cases, which were of such a nature that they could not fail, as time went on, to draw attention to the substantial unity of all payments for the use of capital.

First. The lender had a right to compensation for any loss which he could prove that he had suffered in consequence of the loan. This compensation is the original meaning of our modern term "*interest.*"[2] The right to compensation for the "*damnum emergens*" was first recognised; afterwards also that for the "*lucrum cessans.*" Nothing could be better calculated to establish the common nature of the interest on a person's own trade-capital and on the money he lent to other persons, than this right to compensation for a gain which the lender would have been able to make, had he not lent his money. This became still more evident when, as in Genoa, the opportunity of discounting bills was generally recognised as a ground for claiming the *lucrum cessans.* Thus "interest" more and more became the general term given to payments for business-loans, whilst "usury" was restricted to signify the payment for money-advances made for consumption.

of the Canonists to suppress loans for business purposes; but this concession, though it puts the *practical* policy of the Church in a more favourable light, does not in the least lessen the strength of the argument here advanced. Comp. *Ashley*, loc. cit. p. 437–38.

[1] For fuller account of these cases, see *Cunningham*, The Growth of English Industry and Commerce, Vol. II. Cambridge 1892; *Ashley*, loc. cit.; and especially, *Endemann*, Studien in der Romanisch-Kanonistischen Wirtschafts- und Rechtslehre, Band 2, Berlin 1883.

[2] It was a general rule that "Interesse non debetur nisi ex mora." "The total result of the movement of thought," says *Ashley* (loc. cit. p. 402), "was this: that any merchant . . .

Second. It was a common practice to sell and purchase *rent-charges* on land.[1] This opened up a wide field for the capitalist to make his money productive, and at the same time made it possible for every land-owner to borrow capital at interest. And as agriculture was the main sphere for the use of capital, this form of loan went a long way to clear up popular opinion as to the essential nature of a payment for the advance of money. In Germany, where the purchases of rents were most common, the language adopted the word *Zins* (= census = rent) as the general expression for all recognised forms of payment for loan.

Thus practice had already prepared the ground for a broader view of the problem of interest ; and when finally there came conscious opposition to the interest-policy of the Church, the defenders of the rights of the lenders had little more to do than to remove the dualism between the payment for the simple use of money and the interest on capital, created by mediæval economic policy and defended with mediæval sophistry. Still the quarrel had to go on for more than two centuries before the artificial distinctions of the Canonists were definitely obliterated, the essential unity of the problem recognised, and thus the foundation laid, upon which a scientific theory of interest could be built.

could, with a perfectly clear conscience, and without any fear of molestation, contract to receive periodical interest from a person to whom he lent money ; *provided only* that he first lent it to him gratuitously, for a period which might be made very short, so that technically the payment would not be reward for the use but compensation for the non-return of the money."— A good illustration of mediæval sophistry !

[1] " What was actually sold (in the beginning) was a rent-charge already in existence. . . . From this it was an easy transition to the sale of a rent-charge which had not existed before, but which was first created by the contract ; and this practice speedily became very general " (*Ashley*).

At the same time, the general movement towards freedom of thought began to replace mere appeal to authorities by real investigation and independent thinking.   For the theory of interest, this signified that such quotations as " Mutuum date nihil inde sperantes " from the Bible, or " Pecunia non parit pecuniam " from Aristotle, or later interpretations of such quotations, or meanings read into the Fathers, could no longer be referred to as ultimate grounds for accepting the one or the other opinion about interest.   And thus the exertions of thinkers were directed to the far more fruitful work of investigating the advantages or disadvantages of a low rate, or, generally, the consequences of alterations of the rate.   From this point there is a continuous chain of evolution up to the modern theory of interest.

Thus we may say that the two principal factors which created Modern Times, viz., the economic revolution and the emancipation of thought, also supplied the necessary conditions for a scientific treatment of the problem of interest.

§ 2. *Interest a market price, determined by supply and demand.*

The secular power which at the beginning of Modern Times succeeded the ecclesiastical, soon found it necessary to replace the old *prohibition* by a *regulation* of the rate of interest.   As the old distinctions between different kinds of interest could no longer be maintained, it became necessary to adopt another line of separation between what should be regarded as right and what as wrong in loan-contracts.   And it was very natural to choose a certain fixed rate of interest as drawing this line. Thus we frequently find a maximum rate of interest stipulated in the mediæval Italian republics and in France.   In England Henry VIII. breaking for the first time with the prohibition of interest, decided (1575) that anything under 10 per cent. should be regarded as a fair rate of interest.

Doubtless there were good reasons for a policy which, on this new line, tried to resist the monopoly of the money-lenders, and give the economically weak some protection.   The lover of historical parallels might find an analogy to this policy in the modern programme of a Minimum Rate of Wages, or the " Living Wage."   Certainly this programme corresponds better to the most urgent needs of modern society than does the traditional prohibition of usury which seems again to be attaining popularity in some Continental states.   But, in the sixteenth century, the Fixed Rate of Interest could probably with better right claim a central position in the policy of protecting the weak.   The Fixed Rate must have had a tendency to put an end to that kind of competition which sought to balance every insecurity by a higher rate of interest ; and thus to force lenders to careful selection of the best securities for their loans.   And it would probably be of great interest for a historical student to trace how far this policy aided in "levelling up" the general character of the securities offered, just as we now expect the " Common Rule " to do with the character of labour.[1]

The maximum rate of interest in England was reduced from 10 per cent. to 8 per cent. in 1624, then to 6 per cent. about 1651, confirmed in 1660, and to 5 per cent. under Queen Anne.   A modern mind is disposed to look upon these successive legal reductions of the rate with very much doubt as to their real efficiency and value.   But we should always remember, in dealing with economic life in

[1] Comp. *Sidney and Beatrice Webb*, Industrial Democracy.

those times, that we have not to do with a state of free and highly developed competition, nor with a "market" such as modern economic theory postulates.   Most probably there was a strong tendency, as regards a large part of loan-contracts, to fix the rate of interest at the legal maximum ; and we can imagine that, even in the cases where ultimately a lower rate was stipulated, the bargain began at this maximum as a starting point and was in some degree influenced thereby. In no case can we assume that there was a precisely determinate rate which "demand and supply" would have fixed mechanically, had there been no restrictions upon the market. Thus we must admit the *possibility* that the reductions of the legal rate may have had some real influence in the direction of securing better conditions for the borrowers.[1]   But the probability of such an effect must have diminished very considerably with every new reduction of the rate, and of course it gradually disappeared as trade became more complex and loan-contracts more frequent, *i.e.*, as the ideal conditions of the "market" were gradually realised.

But though we might thus admit that the policy of regulation of interest did, on the whole, work to the advantage of the society of the time, our judgment cannot be the same about its effects on the development of a scientific theory of interest. For the custom of regulating the rate by government edicts made people look upon interest as a thing that could generally be regulated by human will, and diverted public attention from the deeper causes which determine the rate of interest, and which it should be the very object of the theory of interest to explain.   Thus, the earlier writers of the seventeenth century generally limited themselves to discussions about the advantages or disadvantages of a further

[1] Comp. p. 16, note 4.

reduction of the legal rate, without penetrating to the heart of the problem. Still they were able to find some connections between the variations in the rate of interest and other economic phenomena ; and thus some knowledge was gained which became useful as a real theory of interest began in time to develop.

We shall perhaps get the best conception of this change of view if we observe how the problem of interest—which the Canonists had treated "with more wit than wisdom"—presented itself to the genius of *Bacon*. For him it consists in an inquiry into the disadvantages and advantages (observe the order !) of money-lending on interest. On the one side, this system

(*a*) "Diminishes the number of traders on their own capital ;
(*b*) Impoverishes the active merchant ;
(*c*) Contracts the volume of trade, and so of the revenue ;
(*d*) Concentrates wealth in the hands of a few ;
(*e*) Lowers the selling price of land ;
(*f*) Checks manufacturing enterprise ;
(*g*) Eats up old estates."
But on the other side, it
(*a*) "Encourages trade on borrowed capital ;
(*b*) Prevents forced sales and foreclosures ;
(*c*) To abolish interest is to abolish lending altogether."

Bacon concludes that too high a rate of interest should be prohibited ; but there should be left to the capitalist "sufficient inducement to make those advances which are so necessary for the steadiness and the life of commerce."[1]

In the discussions of the following century, *Bacon's* arguments of the first group were frequently used to

[1] Essay of Usury, 1612.

prove the advisability of an abatement of the legal
rate of interest.   Thus *Sir Th. Culpeper* complained
that "the high rate of Usury makes Land sell so
cheape." [1]   And *Sir Josiah Child* returned often in
his writings to this point. [2]   One good result of these
discussions was the statement of the truth that the
rate of interest regulates the number of years'
purchase given for a piece of land.   But *Child*
thought that the real wealth of the kingdom could
be augmented by a reduction of the rate of interest,
and that accordingly such an increase lay within the
immediate reach of governmental power.   And this
evident absurdity, which was sharply criticised by
Thomas Manley,[3] probably did much to clear up
opinions about the objective nature of interest.

Sir Th. Culpeper had taken up the argument that
a high rate of interest (10 per cent.) makes "men
grow lazie in their professions, and become Usurers."[4]
But it was answered, by the friends of freedom of
interest, that this need not diminish the whole
volume of trade ; for the possibility of borrowing
money gives an "opportunity to the *younger and
poorer* Merchants to rise in the world, and to enlarge
their dealings." [5]   *Thomas Manley* answers the

[1] A Tract against Usury.   Presented to the High Court of
Parliament.   London 1621.

[2] Brief Observations concerning Trade and Interest of Money.
London, 1668.—A short Addition to the observations concerning
Trade and Interest of Money.   London 1668.

[3] Interest of Money Mistaken.   Or a Treatise proving, that the
Abatement of *Interest* is the *Effect* and not the *Cause* of the Riches
of a Nation. . . . London 1668.

[4] Loc. cit.   *Child* took the same view : merchants "when they
have gotten great wealth, leave trading " and lend out their money
at interest, "the gain thereof being so easy, certain and great ;
whereas in other countries, where interest is at a lower rate, they
continue merchants from generation to generation, and enrich
themselves and the state."

[5] *Thomas Mun* : England's Treasure by Forraign Trade.   Or
the Ballance of our Forraign Trade is the Rule of our Treasure,

question why cannot the lender just as well make 6 per cent. himself, when the borrower is sup- posed to gain more, by saying : " This were very true, admitting all men were of equall brains and education, to traffick in one sort or other. . . . 'Tis much better for the publick that experienced Traders hire money, and employ it, than sit still, whilst commerce is manag'd by the unskillfull. . . ." [1] This line of thought was fruitful, because it showed that there was a market for the Use of Capital as well as one for Business Ability. And the great Free Trader, *Sir Dudley North*, followed up the idea in these words : " Now as there are more Men to Till the Ground than have Land to Till, so also there will be many who want Stock to manage ; and also (when a Nation is grown rich) there will be Stock for Trade in many hands, who either have not the skill or care not for the trouble of managing it in Trade. But as the Landed Man letts his Land, so these still lett their Stock ; this latter is call'd Interest, but is only Rent for Stock, as the other is for Land." [2]

There was, even in this period, some analysis of the supply and demand side of the capital market. *North* tried to show that the supply of capital must be encouraged by a rise in the rate of interest, and thus entered upon a question which is of the utmost importance for our problem, but on which—even after two centuries of discussion—sufficient light has

London 1664. [Included in the " Early English Tracts on Com- merce," ed. MacCulloch, London 1856 ; Reprint, Macmillan and Co. 1895].

[1] *Th. Manley* : Usury at six per cent. examined, and found unjustly charged by Sir Th. Culpeper, and J. C., with many Crimes and Oppressions, whereof 'tis altogether innocent.

[2] *Sir Dudley North* : Discourses upon Trade ; principally directed to the Cases of the Interest, Coynage, Clipping, and Increase of Money. London 1691. [In the " Early English Tracts on Commerce," ed. MacCulloch, London 1856] p. 517.

not been thrown. *North* remarks that "high Interest will bring Money out from Hoards, Plate, &c., into Trade, when low Interest will keep it back . . . So that it cannot be denied but the lowering of Interest may, and probably will, keep some Money from coming abroad into Trade ; whereas on the contrary high Interest certainly brings it out."[1]   Far deeper into the very heart of the problem of the supply of capital entered the clear-sighted *Sir William Petty.*[2]   He saw that there must be some relation between the period of time for which human beings generally could be supposed to provide and the rate of interest.   And though he did not grasp the whole bearing of this idea, later theorists on interest would have done well to pay more attention to his reasoning.   The following quotation will give its essence : "Having found the Rent or value of the *usus fructus per annum*, the question is, how many years purchase . . . is the Fee simple naturally worth ? "   As it cannot be infinite "we must pitch upon some limited number, and that I apprehend to be the number of years, which I conceive one man of fifty years old, another of twenty-eight, and another of seven years old, all being alive together may be thought to live ; that is to say, of a Grandfather, Father, and Child ; few men having reason to take care of more remote Posterity : for if a man be a great Grandfather, he himself is so much nearer his end, so as there are but three in a continual line of descent usually co-existing together ; and as some are Grandfathers at forty years, yet as many are not till above sixty, and *sic de cæteris.*"

"Wherefore I pitch the number of years purchase, that any Land is naturally worth, to be the ordinary extent of three such persons their lives.   Now in *England* we esteem three lives equal to one and twenty

[1] Loc. cit., p. 519–520.
[2] A Treatise of Taxes and Contributions.   London 1667.

years, and consequently the value of Land, to be about the same number of years purchase. Possibly if they thought themselves mistaken in the one (as the observator of the Bills of Mortality thinks they are), they would alter in the other, unless the consideration of the force of popular error and dependence of things already concatenated, did hinder them." Hence he concludes that "the least (the natural standard of Usury) can be, is the Rent of so much Land as the money lent will buy."

What principally occupied the economists of the seventeenth century was, however, not the supply side of the capital-market, but the demand side, *i.e.*, from their point of view, the influence of variations of the rate of interest upon the volume of trade. *Sir Thomas Culpeper* remarked that every business, enterprise or invention which promised to yield *less* than ten per cent. on the capital invested was prohibited under a rate of interest of ten per cent.[1] And the younger *Sir Thomas Culpeper*,[2] taking up this argument, concluded that an abatement of the legal rate will enable improvements in agriculture and "revive our dying Manufacture." The advocates of free interest recognised this effect of a high rate, but they tried to show that the real order of cause and effect was the reverse : "as plenty makes cheapness in other things, as Corn, Wool, &c., when they come to Market in greater Quantities than there are Buyers to deal for, the Price will fall ; so if there be more Lenders than Borrowers, Interest will also fall ; wherefore it is not low Interest makes Trade, but Trade increasing, the Stock of the Nation makes Interest low."[3] However, *Thomas Mun* seems to have arrived at a fairly clear con-

[1] Loc. cit.
[2] A Discourse shewing the many Advantages which will accrue to this Kingdom by the abatement of *Usury*. London 1668.
[3] *Sir Dudley North*, loc. cit.

ception of the mutual dependence of both factors, and is thus in advance of many economists of our own day.[1]

Though the original object of all these discussions was to state the probable effects of alterations in the rate of interest, they could not but create and gradually develop a new conception of the nature of interest itself.   Every new insight into the connexion between the rate and other economic factors pointed to the fact that interest was in reality influenced and determined by these factors ;   and thus could no longer be looked upon as a matter of deliberate policy, but as an objective phenomenon of economic life.   This view manifests itself in the expression "natural," which from this time plays a prominent, though not always a fortunate part in writings on political economy, meaning by that a state of things not influenced by legal restrictions. *Sir William Petty's* ideas on this matter had already attained a remarkable maturity :   his words "the vanity and fruitlessness of making Civil Positive Laws against the Laws of Nature" are an acute expression of his view.[2]   *Th. Manley* maintains "the natural lowness

[1] England's Treasure, p. 179.   "We might conclude, contrary to those who affirm, that Trade decreaseth as Usury encreaseth, for they *rise and fall together*."—Yet *Child* maintained his view [A New Discourse of Trade, 2nd Ed. London 1694] : "I think it will be out of doubt, that abatement of Interest is the Cause of increase of the Trade and Riches of any Kingdom."   He gives himself much trouble to show that this had been the case in Holland also ; and though the Dutch had not at that time any legal restriction of interest, he held that they had made it their "policy" to keep their rate of interest three or four per cent. lower than in other countries !

[2] Loc. cit.   *Petty* places interest on the same footing with agio in exchange : "Now the questions arising hence are : what are the natural Standards of Usury and Exchange?   As for Usury, the least that can be is the Rent of so much Land as the money lent will buy, where the security is undoubted ; but where the security is casual, then a kind of ensurance must be enterwoven with the simple natural Interest, which may advance the Usury very con-

of Interest to be the effects of riches."[1]   And we
have already seen how clearly *North* stated his
views on interest as a market price; an idea which
he emphasizes in speaking of the "universal
Maxime, that as more Buyers than Sellers raiseth
the price of a commodity, so more Borrowers than
Lenders will raise Interest;" or of "the Price, which
the Reason of Trade settles."[2]   In the same year as
North's work was published, *John Locke* wrote his
"Considerations of the consequences of the lowering of interest and raising the value of money,"
where he showed himself a decided advocate of the
new view.[3]   From that time all serious investigations
into our problem started with the assumption of a
market, where the rate of interest was determined by

scionably unto any height below the Principal itself."   This is
indeed a remarkable instance of acute analysis of the nature of
interest.   *Petty* takes up the comparison with exchange in his
"Quantulumcunque concerning Money" (written 1682, publ.
London 1695; Select Collection of scarce and valuable Tracts
on Money; ed. MacCulloch, London 1856): "Qu. 28. *What is
Interest or Use-Money?   Answ.* A Reward for forbearing the use
of your own Money for a Term of Time agreed upon, whatsoever
need you self may have of it in the mean while.   Qu. 29. *What
is Exchange?   Answ.* Local Interest, or a Reward given for having
your Money at such a Place where you most need the use of it."
The same parallel is used by *Rice Vaughan*: A Discourse of coin
and coinage; the first Invention and Use of Money, London
1675 [in the above named Collection]: "there are many kinds
(of usury) of which the most refined is that of *Exchange*, which is
mix'd with an usury of place, as that is of time."
   [1] *Manley*: Interest of Money Mistaken.
   [2] *North*: loc. cit. p. 522.
   [3] Works, Vol. V. London 1823, p. 7: "But that law cannot
keep men from taking more use than you set (the want of money
being that alone which regulates its price) will perhaps appear, if
we consider how . . . impossible it is to set a rate upon victuals,
in a time of famine; for money being an universal commodity, and
as necessary to trade as food is to life, everybody must have it, at
what rate that they can get it; and unavoidably pay dear, when it
is scarce."—p. 67: it is impossible through the method of legal
enactment to reduce interest under "the natural rate of interest."

demand and supply. Thus the discussion on interest
had already in the seventeenth century taken its
stand on the general ideas which later on took
shape in the economic theory of Free Trade.

We should have no adequate grasp of this whole
discussion if we assumed the advocates of legal
restrictions to have absolutely neglected the influence
of objective economic factors upon the rate of
interest. *Sir Th. Culpeper* thought that an abatement of the legal rate would increase trade and
therefore "money;" "and it is the plenty of money
within the Land that maketh money easy to be
borrowed;" he thought also that the abatement
would diminish the number of borrowers; and on
these grounds it would be *possible* to *maintain* the
lower rate.[1] *Sir Jos. Child* holds that "the matter
in England is prepared for an abatement of Interest;"[2] and he is so far from ignoring the forces
of "nature," that he expressly states: "Nature
must and will have its course;" and even quotes
the authority of *Petty* for this sentence.[3] And a
century later such a decided advocate of the freedom
of interest as *Sir James Steuart* showed himself
clear-sighted and fair enough to recognise that the
legal abatements of the rate in England might have
had some real effect.[4]

[1] A Tract against Usury, etc.
[2] Brief Observations, etc.
[3] In the "Suppliment."—Compare also *Th. Manley's* reply to
these authors (Usury at six per cent., etc., Preface) where he
denies that matters were prepared for an abatement of the rate :
the Dutch "have nothing hinders their taking 20 per cent. but
their vast riches, and prosperity : but here with us, and in all
countries where money is scarce, how difficult is it to restrain
interest within its legall bounds, not occasioned, surely, so much
through the rapine and severity of the lender, as by reason of the
scarcity of money, and multitude of borrowers ; so ripe are affairs
with us to be wedded to higher interest, and so fervent nature is
to have its course."
[4] An Inquiry into the Principle of Political Œconomy, London

§ 3. *Interest paid for the use of Capital, not for the use of Money.*

Once it was recognised that Interest was a price, determined like all other prices by demand and supply, three different subjects naturally presented themselves for further investigation, viz. :

(*a*) The mechanism of the market, where supply and demand meet to determine interest ; and the nature of the factors operating,

(*b*) on the Supply Side,

(*c*) on the Demand Side of that market.

In the next period of the history of our problem, which, broadly speaking, may be said to be that of the eighteenth century, the investigations as to the first subject were far more successful than seems to have been generally recognised. There was besides some vagueness in the idea of interest which had to be removed ; and in this period two important steps were taken to do this, and thus to arrive at a more accurate and definite conception of the very subject of the discussion.

The first of these steps was to disentangle the old confusion between *money* and *capital*. As loans are generally made in money, it was very natural to look upon material money as the essential object of the transaction, and to ascribe the variations in the rate of interest to its abundance or scarcity. Hence such expressions as "cheap" and "dear" money,

1767. It is an essential condition for a market-rate that borrowing is "frequent and familiar." "Were we to suppose a state, where borrowing and lending are not common, and where the laws fix no determinate interest for money, it would hardly be possible to ascertain the rate of it at any time." This was the case in old times . . . "It was impossible for any statesman to determine any just rate of interest" (p. 116 etc.).

which still remain familiar in the language of commerce and banking. According to *Locke*, interest is paid for the "use of money." "In money there is a double value": (*a*) "it is capable, by its interest, to yield . . . a yearly income : and in this it has the nature of land ;" (*b*) "it is capable, by exchange, to procure" commodities : "and in this it has the nature of a commodity."[1] "The natural value of money, as it is apt to yield such a yearly income by interest, depends on the whole quantity of the then passing money of the kingdom, in proportion to the whole trade of the kingdom, *i.e.* the general vent of all the commodities. But the natural value of money, in exchanging for any one commodity, is the quantity of the trading money of the kingdom designed for that commodity, in proportion to that single commodity and its vent."[2] Very much the same view was taken by *Montesquieu*. He saw that interest was a price determined by supply and demand, but he thought that money was the essential object of the bargain, and called interest the "price of money."[3] The same misapprehension made the elder *Mirabeau* fall back upon the old condemnation of interest on the ground of the "barrenness" of money. He calls the laws of Mercantilism for

[1] *Locke*, Some Considerations, etc. p. 33–34.

[2] *Ibid.* p. 46.

[3] *Montesquieu*, Œuvres Complètes, ed. *Laboulaye*, Paris, 1877. T. 5. Esprit des Lois, Livre XXII. ch. VI. : "L'Inca Garcilasso dit qu'en Espagne, après la conquête des Indes, les rentes, qui étoient au denier dix, tombèrent au denier vingt. Cela devoit être ainsi. Une grande quantité d'argent fut tout à coup portée en Europe : bientôt moins de personnes eurent besoins d'argent ; le prix de toutes choses augmenta, et celui de l'argent diminua ; la proportion fut donc rompue, toutes les anciennes dettes furent éteintes. On peut se rappeler le temps du Système (Law), où toutes les choses avoient une grande valeur, excepté l'argent. Après la conquête des Indes, ceux qui avoient de l'argent furent obligés de diminuer le prix ou le louage de leur marchandise, c'est à dire, l'intérêt."

retaining money in the country ridiculous; the nature of money is to serve as an instrument for bargaining; but money has no *other* value, and therefore it is wrong to claim interest.[1]

David Hume seems to have been the first to bring light into this confusion.[2] He remarks that "Lowness of interest is generally ascribed to plenty of money," and tries to disprove this opinion: "Were gold rendered as common as silver, and silver as common as copper, would money be more plentiful, or interest lower?" No . . . "unless we imagine that the colour of the metal is of any consequence." "The greater or less quantity of (money) in a state has no influence on the interest. But it is evident that the greater or less stock of labour and commodities must have a great influence; since we really and in effect borrow these, when we take money upon interest." Here a distinction was made, which proved to be of the highest importance for the further development of the theory of interest. This theory has since proceeded on the assumption that money is merely an arbitrary form for loans with which interest has nothing to do, and that this form may therefore be neglected in investigations into the causes governing the *Capital* market. No doubt this hypothesis has been very fruitful by isolating the problem of interest from that of money, but it now seems time that we should ask ourselves how far it is consistent with the facts. Already *Hume*

[1] *Victor Riquetti, Marquis de Mirabeau,* Philosophie Rurale, Amsterdam, 1766, Ch. VI.: "L'attachement que la détention forcée inspire pour ce métal dans les Nations, le fait paroître plus précieux que sa valeur de compensation avec les autres richesses, et provoque le goût de l'avarice, l'ennemie secrette du fisc. Il devient rare en conséquence, et dès-lors, au lieu de l'avoir en échange, pour le donner de même, ce qui est sa vraie fonction, il faut l'acheter pour s'en procurer l'usage."

[2] Essays, Moral, Political, and Literary. Part II. (publ. 1752); Essay IV. Of Interest. [Works, London, 1826.]

had seen that it was not. He says : "All augmentation (of the quantity of money) has no other effect than to heighten the price of labour and commodities. . . . In the progress towards these changes, the augmentation may have some influence, by exciting industry ; but after the prices are settled, suitable to the new abundance of gold and silver, it has no manner of influence." This clear distinction between dynamic and static conditions, between a state of movement and a state of equilibrium seems to do the highest credit to the analytical power of *Hume* ; certainly our modern science would gain much if it observed this distinction more strictly. And if it is true that the use of money materially alters the conditions of the problem of interest, we would do well not to claim for our present theories that they are more than preliminaries to a theory of real interest as we find it in the actual market.

It would only be fair to the earlier authors to recognise that they were in their circumstances right in ascribing to the quantity of money some influence on the rate of interest ;[1] though they generally gave this influence too prominent a place in their explanation of interest, and even misunderstood its character.

The question, For what is interest paid ? was taken up again, a few years afterwards, and treated in the most successful way, by the eminent French economist *Turgot*. He rejects the old idea of a " price of money " and defines interest as *the price given for the use of a certain quantity of value during a certain time*—a formula never afterwards

[1] Comp. *Steuart*, loc. cit. Book IV. Ch. 7 : "A statesman has it in his power to increase or diminish the extent of credit and paper money in circulation, by various expedients, which greatly influence the rate of interest " . . . "interest falls in proportion to the redundancy of money to be lent."

surpassed in clearness and definiteness.[1] He shows how this price is fixed by demand and supply,[2] and he gives special attention to the causes which govern the *demand* for capital. What he has to say on this subject is, even in our days, of the highest value, and should not be neglected by any serious student of the theory of interest. He puts capital, *i.e.* the use of a certain quantity of value during a certain time, as a factor of production on the same line with the other factors, and he shows in the most brilliant way how the extension which a nation can give to its enterprises of agriculture, industry, and commerce, is limited by the current rate of interest.[3] He knows that a buyer of

---

[1] Sur la Formation et la Distribution des Richesses (1766) [Œuvres de Turgot T fig. 1, Paris 1844].

§ 78. "Au marché, une mesure de blé se balance avec un certain poids d'argent ; c'est une quantité d'argent qu'on achète avec la denrée ; c'est cette quantité qu'on apprécie et qu'on compare avec d'autres valeurs étrangères.—Dans le prêt à l'intérêt, l'objet de l'appréciation est l'usage d'une certaine quantité de valeurs pendant un certain temps. Ce n'est plus une masse d'argent qu'on compare à une masse de blé ; c'est une masse de valeurs qu'on compare avec une portion déterminée d'elle-même, qui devient le prix de l'usage de cette masse pendant un certain temps."

[2] "J'ai déjà dit que l'intérêt de l'argent prêté se réglait, comme celui de toutes les autres marchandises, par la balance de l'offre à la demande. Ainsi, quand il y a beaucoup d'emprunteurs qui ont besoin d'argent, l'intérêt de l'argent devient plus haut ; quand il y a beaucoup de possesseurs d'argent qui en offrent à prêter, l'intérêt baisse" (§ 75).

[3] § 88. "Si l'intérêt est à cinq pour cent, toute terre à défricher, dont les produits ne rapporteront pas cinq pour cent, outre le remplacement des avances et la récompense des soins du cultivateur, restera en friche ; toute fabrique, tout commerce qui ne rapporteront pas cinq pour cent, outre le salaire des peines et les risques de l'entrepreneur, n'existeront pas."

§ 89. "On peut regarder le prix de l'intérêt comme une espèce de niveau au-dessous duquel tout travail, toute culture, toute industrie, tout commerce cessent. C'est comme une mer répandue sur une vaste contrée : les sommets des montagnes s'élèvent au-dessus des eaux, et forment des îles fertiles et cultivées. Si

land does not increase the demand for capital ; that this demand is increased only by economic progress. He thoroughly understands the mutual dependence of the various factors in the problem and goes perhaps deepest when he points to the competition of the various branches of production for the use of capital.[1]

Of course it was impossible for *Turgot*, in dealing with this side of the problem, not to state that capital cannot be used in industry, unless it yields at least the same rent as the capitalist is able to secure for himself by buying land.   Out of this a modern Austrian critic, *Böhm-Bawerk*, has constructed what he calls a " fructification theory of interest "—the theory that the possibility of gaining rent from land is the *cause* of interest—and has thus made it easy for himself to pass over the profound investigation of one of the greatest geniuses who worked in our science in the eighteenth century as hardly more than a simple confusion of thought.[2] [3] It indeed may be doubted whether such criticism is more discreditable to the author himself or to those students who have accepted him as an authority without taking even the simplest precautions to obtain confirmation of his statements.

cette mer vient à s'écouler, à mesure qu'elle descend, les terrains en pente, puis les plaines et les vallons, paraissent et se couvrent de productions de toute espèce.   Il suffit que l'eau monte ou s'abaisse d'un pied pour inonder ou pour rendre à la culture de plages immenses."

[1] § 83. " Il est évident que les produits annuels qu'on peut retirer des capitaux placés dans ces différents emplois sont bornés les uns par les autres, et tous relatifs au taux actuel de l'intérêt de l'argent."

[2] The present writer is indebted to *Prof. Marshall* for some very suggestive remarks on this point.

[3] *E. von Böhm-Bawerk*, Geschichte und Kritik der Kapitalzinstheorien.   1st ed. Innsbruck 1884 ; 2d ed. 1900.   The quotations in the following are from the English translation by *Prof. Smart ;* but the second German edition has been consulted.

Adam Smith does not seem to have added anything of special importance to the theory of interest. But he stated the results already won in simple and clear language and gave them the whole weight of his authority ; and these results accordingly were, from his time, accepted as definite. He placed himself entirely at the point of view of natural science as opposed to the old view of economic policy, and tried to inquire, generally, into the "nature and causes of the wealth of nations," and, specially, into those of interest. He looked on the problem of interest as essentially a problem of price ; [1] and thus it was enough for him to state that interest is necessary.

(*a*) in order to call forth a sufficient *supply* of capital ; [2]

(*b*) because the necessity of advances leads to a never ceasing *demand* for capital. [3]

On neither of these points was his analysis very profound ; but his different explanations were in consistence with one another and with the general conception of interest as a market-price. The dis-

---

[1] "As the quantity of stock to be lent at interest increases, the interest, or the price which must be paid for the use of that stock, necessarily diminishes." [Wealth of Nations II., 4.] "When the stocks of many rich merchants are turned into the same trade their mutual competition naturally tends to lower its profits ; and when there is a like increase of stock in all the different trades carried on in the same society, the same competition must produce the same effect in them all" [ibid. I. 9].

[2] "Something must be given for the profits of the undertaker of the work, who hazards his stocks in this adventure. . . . He could have no interest to employ them, unless he expected from the sale of their work something more than what was sufficient to replace his stock to him" [ibid. I. 6].

[3] "In all arts and manufactures the greater part of the workmen stand in need of a master to advance them the materials of their work, and their wages and maintenance till it be completed" [ibid. I. 8].

tinction between the problem of interest and that of
money was upheld by *Smith* with his usual clearness,[1] and here, as in the question of the influence
of interest upon the value of land, he took very
much the same position as *Turgot*.[2]

§ 4. *Subdivision of Profits into Interest and "Profits of Enterprise."*

It had been the rule to use the term " Profits " to
denote the total net earnings of a business man irrespective of whether these were to be ascribed to his capital
or to other sources.   On this point a deeper analysis
was necessary for a successful study of *pure interest*
and of the causes which determine it.   It would be
misleading to suppose that the earlier economists
did not understand the difference between business-
profits in general and that part of them which is
properly interest on capital ; *Adam Smith* tells us
expressly that, in his time, double interest was
considered a fair rate of profit.[3]   But they did not
carry out this distinction consistently,   and they

[1] " Almost all loans at interest are made in money, either of
paper, or of gold and silver ; but what the borrower really wants,
and what the lender really supplies him with, is not the money,
but the money's worth, or the goods which it can purchase . . .
By means of the loan, the lender, as it were, assigns to the
borrower his right to a certain portion of the annual produce
of the land and labour of the country, to be employed as the
borrower pleases.   The quantity of stock, therefore, or, as it is
commonly expressed, of money which can be lent at interest in
any country, is not regulated by the value of the money, whether
paper or coin, which serves as the instrument of the different
loans made in that country " [ibid. II. 4].
[2] " The ordinary market price of land . . . depends everywhere
upon the ordinary market rate of interest " ; but there are some
reasons why people generally content themselves with less interest
when buying land [ibid. II. 4].
[3] Wealth of Nations, I. 9.

never isolated the problem of pure interest. Under such circumstances, it was of course impossible to arrive at an accurate analysis of the factors which operate either on the demand side or on the supply side in determining the rate of interest.

The credit of having introduced the conception of pure interest into the science is due to *J. B. Say*.[1] He separated the functions of the capitalist from those of the "*entrepreneur*," capital from business ability, and interest from the reward of such ability. In England these distinctions were immediately adopted by *Tooke*,[2] but it was a long time before they completely took hold of English economic literature, and we may, even in our days, trace the insufficient analysis of the earlier economists in the fact that the English language has no adequate word for the French "*entrepreneur*" or the German "*Unternehmer*."

Say has also given a very complete and profound analysis of the mechanism of the market in which interest is determined, and thus provided the general scheme into which every explanation of particular points or sides of our problem must be fitted as parts of an organic whole. Therefore, to get an adequate idea of what *Say* has done for the theory of interest, it is necessary to go back to his general price-theory.

In this theory the ideas of the Free-Trade-school as to the process by which prices are governed, may be said to have found their classical expression. *Say* starts from the wants of the individual, as these

[1] Traité d'économie politique. The three first editions of this famous work were issued in 1803, 1814, and 1817 ; in the last of these important alterations were made. The quotations in the following are from the edition issued by Say's son in 1841 (Paris).
[2] *Tooke*, History of Prices, Vol. II., London 1838 ; p. 357. [This passage is extracted from the "Considerations on the State of the Currency," which were published in 1826].

are expressed in his will and his capacity to pay for the means of satisfying them. As a matter of fact, every individual makes a certain classification of his wants, liable to alterations according to the variation of prices. Thus a certain *demand* is created for every article, and as this quantity varies with the price, there is no sense in speaking about demand without adding : at this or that price.[1] The means of satisfying the wants are produced by a process, of which the elementary factors are the " productive services," viz.: *personal* services, the service of *land*

[1] Loc. cit. Livre II., Ch. I. *Say* has common sense enough not to trouble himself, in an economic investigation, with the physiological or psychical causes of human wants : " Nous ne considérons encore ces besoins que comme des *quantités données*, sans en rechercher les causes."—" Chaque individu, ou chaque famille . . . sont obligés de faire une sorte de classement de leurs besoins pour satisfaire ceux auxquels ils attachent plus d'importance, préférablement à ceux auxquels ils en attachent moins. . . . Nous ne considérons encore ce classement que comme une chose de fait et d'observation." . . . " De là naît pour chaque produit une certaine quantité recherchée et demandée en chaque lieu, quantité qui est modifiée par le prix auquel il peut être fourni ; car plus il revient cher au producteur en raison des frais de production dont il est le résultat, et plus, dans la classification qu'en font les consommateurs, il est reculé, et se voit préférer tous les produits capables de procurer une satisfaction plus grand pour le même prix."—When the price rises, " non seulement le nombre de consommateurs diminue, mais chaque consommateur réduit sa consommation. Il est tel consommateur de café qui, lorsque cette denrée hausse de prix, peut n'être pas forcé de renoncer entièrement aux douceurs de ce breuvage. Il réduira seulement sa provision accoutumée. . . . "—" Telles sont les causes générales qui bornent la quantité de chaque chose qui peut être demandée. Et comme cette quantité varie suivant le prix auquel elle peut être offerte, on voit que l'on ne doit jamais parler de quantité demandée sans exprimer ou supposer convenue cette restriction : au prix où l'on peut se la procurer."—It is difficult to see what the modern theory of final or marginal utility, and particularly that of the Austrian school, has added, of real value for the theory of prices, to this clear statement of the demand as a *function* of the price ; but we shall see later on how much inferior the Austrian school is in giving an adequate account of the general mechanism of the market.

and the service of *capital.* The demand of every individual for a commodity is limited by the amount of services he can afford to give in exchange. The supply of the commodity is limited by its *cost of production.* This is the aggregate value of all services necessary for the production of the commodity. No commodity can long be produced at a lower price, and thus the price of a commodity depends on the cost of production. But, on the other hand, the demand for a special article is ultimately a demand for the special productive services which are required for putting it on the market; and thus the value of the productive services, and consequently that of the commodity itself depends on the demand.[1] To have, in this general manner, for the first time, stated *the mutual dependence of demand, price, and cost of production* does the greatest honour to *J. B. Say.* Unfortunately the importance and the real bearing of this discovery have not been sufficiently recognised, and thus an immense amount of work has been wasted, particularly in the latter part of the nineteenth century, on controversies as to the order of cause and effect which a more thorough study of the work of *Say* would have made superfluous.

After this it is clear that *all* prices, those of the commodities as well as those of the productive services, are regulated by *one and the same market.*

---

[1] "Ainsi, lorsque quelques auteurs, comme *David Ricardo*, ont dit que c'étaient les frais de production qui réglaient la valeur des produits, ils ont eu raison en ce sens, que jamais les produits ne sont vendus d'une manière suivie à un prix inférieur à leurs frais de production ; mais quand ils ont dit que la demande qu'on fait des produits n'influait pas sur leur valeur, ils ont eu, ce me semble, tort en ceci, que la demande influe sur la valeur des services productifs, et, en augmentant les frais de production, élève la valeur des produits sans pour cela qu'elle dépasse les frais de production." [Ibid. p. 322 ; comp. Cours complet d'économie politique, Tome IV., Paris 1829; pp. 149–150].

In this market, the possessors of the productive services are the sellers; the consumers of the products, the buyers.[1] The demand for each special service is *the one base* of its value; the supply of it, varying according to different motives, is the *other base*.

It is now time to look at the position of interest in this process of price-determination. After having, in a somewhat too absolute manner, cleared interest from the influence of money,[2] and also from the element of an insurance premium for risk, *Say* proceeds to isolate *the function of the capitalist*, whom he defines as "*the person who makes the advances*."[3] *What* is advanced, he describes, in the words already used by *Turgot*, as a certain sum of *value*.[4] Now such advances are, as a matter of fact,

[1] "Les raisons qui déterminent la valeur des choses. . . . s'appliquent indifféremment à toutes les choses qui ont une valeur" —therefore also—"aux services productifs que rendent l'industrie, les capitaux et les terres dans l'acte de la production. Ceux qui disposent de l'une de ces trois sources de la production sont marchands de cette denrée que nous appelons ici *services productifs;* les consommateurs des produits en sont les acheteurs." [Livre II., Ch. V. p. 349].

[2] Traité d'économie politique, II. 8; p. 396: "C'est donc bien à tort qu'on se sert du mot *intérêt de l'argent* . . . *Law, Montesquieu,* et le judicieux *Locke* lui-même . . . s'y sont trompés. . . . La théorie de l'intérêt est demeurée couverte d'un voile épais jusqu'à *Hume* et *Smith* qui l'ont levé."—"Le fait est que l'abondance ou la rareté de l'argent, de la monnaie, ou de tout ce qui en tient lieu n'influe *pas du tout* sur le taux de l'intérêt, pas plus que l'abondance ou la rareté de la cannelle, du froment, ou des étoffes de soie." [p. 394].

[3] La portion retirée par le capitaliste, par celui qui a fait des avances, quelque petites et quelque courtes qu'elles aient été, s'appelle *profit du capital*." [p. 351].

[4] "L'intérêt des capitaux prêtés, mal à propos nommé *intérêt de l'argent*, s'appelait auparavant *usure* (loyer de l'usage, de la jouissance), et c'était le mot propre, puisque l'intérêt est un prix, un loyer qu'on paie pour avoir la jouissance d'une valeur." [p. 384].

"Ce qu'on prête est une valeur accumulée et consacrée à un placement." [p. 394].

necessary for all production, and are, therefore, one of the productive services whose prices are determined in the general market.[1] This is in short *Say's* theory of interest ; it is, as we see, the groundwork of a theory, and, as such, of the highest value ; but it left to coming generations a vast field of work in exploring the special causes which determine the supply and demand of that particular service called advance of capital.

§ 5. *Interruption of the Development of the Theory of Interest.*

Realising that a general theory of demand and supply was not enough to explain the actual rate of interest, *Ricardo* proceeded to find some particular *quantitative* relations between the different factors influencing the capital-market. Laying much stress upon the natural tendency of population to increase along with the means of subsistence, he thought that the wages of labour were, practically, fixed between very narrow limits. Further, the product of agriculture on the worst land taken into cultivation, the *marginal* agriculture, had to be shared between the labourer and the capitalist. And as the labourer had to get his traditional necessaries of life, the share of the capitalist seemed to be fairly well determined by the natural productivity of the marginal land. As population increases, this productivity decreases, and consequently the " profits " decrease. But " as soon as wages should be equal to . . . . the whole receipts of the farmer, there must

[1] " L'impossibilité d'obtenir aucun produit sans le concours d'un capital met les consommateurs dans l'obligation de payer, pour chaque produit, un prix suffisant pour que l'entrepreneur qui se charge de sa production, puisse acheter le service de cet instrument nécessaire." [p. 383].

be an end of accumulation ; for no capital can then
yield any profit whatever, and no additional labour
can be demanded, and consequently population will
have reached its highest point. Long, indeed, before
this period, the very low rate of profits will have
arrested all accumulation." And again : " Long
before this state of prices was become permanent,
there would be no motive for accumulation ; for no
one accumulates but with a view to make his accumulation productive " ; and the " motive for accumulation will diminish with every diminution of
profit." [1]

Malthus objected to *Ricardo* that he exaggerated
the adjustment of population to the means of subsistence ; the shares of labour and capital always depend
on their relative *scarceness ;* " when capital is really
abundant compared with labour, profits must be
low, and no facility of production can occasion high
profits, unless capital is scarce." [2] Had any one at

[1] *Ricardo*, Principles of Political Economy, ed. MacCulloch,
Ch. VI. Comp. *Böhm-Bawerk's* criticism of *Ricardo* : " That the
claims of capital may exert this limiting influence *Ricardo* himself
allows, as we have seen, in the very extreme case where profit
threatens to disappear altogether. But naturally those circumstances to which capital owes its existence in general put forth
their energies not only in the very extreme cases, but permanently.
They do not simply prevent the entire disappearance of profit ;
they keep it constantly in competition with the other factors, and
help to determine its amount. So that profit no less than wages
may be said to rest on independent determining grounds. To
have entirely ignored these grounds is the decisive blunder of
Ricardo." (Capital and Interest, p. 94.)

[2] *Malthus*, Principles of Political Economy, London 1820 ;
Summary.—*Malthus'* theory of interest must be looked upon as
a part of his general theory of prices, which is built on a broad
view of the mechanism of the market. The different factors of
production are paid " on account of their rarity, and the consequent rarity of the effects produced by them." Distribution is a
side only of the general process by which prices are fixed. The
price of a product is the sum of the prices of the means of production, " the price of each of these component parts being
determined exactly by the same causes as those which determine

that time understood how to sum up the results of
this discussion between *Ricardo* and *Malthus*, he
might have done it in three points :

Interest is determined by the principle of supply
and demand ;

The supply is regulated by the tendency of accumulation to diminish when the rate of interest
diminishes ;

The demand is regulated by the tendency of
the natural productivity of land to diminish
when the population increases.

The two latter of these would have been good
starting points for further investigations into the
forces operating on the supply and demand of
capital.   Unfortunately the continuity of the development was now interrupted for a long time.
Malthus had a good conception of the mechanism
of the market, and had grasped the mutual dependence of the different factors operating in it ; and
though he did not perhaps state these ideas in so
definite a form as *J. B. Say*, yet he gave them a
very prominent place in his theory of political
economy.   Just the opposite was the case with
Ricardo : the average careless reader was very
likely to overlook what he had to say about supply
and demand, and to take his statements about the
natural standard of wages and profits in a far more
absolute sense than the author had intended to
give them.   It was the greatest of misfortunes, as
regards the further development of economic science,
that *Malthus'* " Principles of Political Economy "
were soon left in the background ; whilst those of

---

the price of the whole." It is obvious, therefore, "that we cannot get rid of the principle of demand and supply by referring to
the cost of production." Interest is the "remuneration for that
part of the production contributed by the capitalist, estimated
exactly in the same way as the contribution of the labourer," *i.e.*
according to the principle of demand and supply.

Ricardo succeeded in winning an exceptional authority. And the carelessness with which *Ricardo* was
read was extraordinary.

Thus it happened that the former steady progress
of the theory of interest was now interrupted for
half a century, serious investigation being replaced
by two theoretical systems, diverging greatly from
one another, but alike in that they were both founded
on mere empty speculation and that both claimed
the authority of *Ricardo*. The one of these systems
is what has been called "scientific" Socialism.

Ricardo had discussed a hypothetical state of
things, where the "use of capital," necessary for the
production of any commodity, was strictly proportional to the labour wanted, and where therefore
the *value* of any commodity was proportional to, and
measured by, the quantity of labour bestowed upon
it on the margin of production. This highly artificial hypothesis was accepted by the Socialists,
omitting all the reservations which *Ricardo* had by
no means failed to state ; and the central formula
of the Ricardian theory of value was falsely given
out to mean that the value of any commodity was
equal to the quantity of labour bestowed upon it.[1]
Gradually the word *value* was alienated from its
original meaning of a virtual *price*, and with *Marx*
it seems rather to signify some kind of mystical fluid
passed into the materia by labour and by labour
alone. But if labour made up the whole of the
value of any commodity, there was of course no
room left for the capitalists' claim of a share in that

---

[1] " Wealth is produced by labor : no other ingredient but labor
makes any object of desire an object of wealth. Labor is the
sole universal measure, as well as the characteristic distinction of
wealth." *William Thompson* : An Inquiry into the principles of
the Distribution of Wealth most conducive to Human Happiness.
London 1824.—Among non-socialistic writers, *MacCulloch* seems
to have contributed most to this false interpretation of the theory
of *Ricardo*.

value ; and it is difficult to understand why the Socialists troubled themselves with further demonstrations of the wrongness of interest.

Marshall has pointed out that history partially repeated itself in the attempt of the Socialists to defend the poor against the capitalists in the field of *production*, just as the Canonists had defended them against being overcharged in loans for *consumption*.[1] It may be added that history repeated itself also in respect to the two principal *methods* used by the Canonists : appeal to authorities, and sophistry. The absolute confidence and the complete lack of criticism with which the Socialists appealed to the authority of *Ricardo* in the question of the nature of value, or, later on, to that of *Marx* in general, were never surpassed by the Mediæval Church when claiming the authority of *Aristotle* or of the Bible. And as for mystic phrases and sophistical reasoning, *Marx* recalls to one's mind the worst of what the scholastic age produced. It is indeed deplorable that such methods should be looked upon as the criterion of "scientific Socialism," as the Germans still love to call it.

Other Socialists repeated other faults with which this survey of history has already made us familiar. The most common of these was to look on interest as a mere outcome of the monetary system. To do away with money was the great aim of the "exchange-banque" of *Proudhon ;* by such means he promised to save the people "the discount" to the amount of 400 million francs, and the mortgage rent of about 1,200 million francs, which otherwise would have to be paid to "monetary parasitism"; and thus in the future "the peasant would borrow at the same rate at which the merchant would discount, *i.e.* gratuitously."[2]

[1] Principles of Economics, Vol. I., 4th Ed. Book VI. Ch. VI. § 3.
[2] *Proudhon*, Résumé de la question sociale, Banque d'Échange (1849).

There is, however, one point in the socialistic writings on interest which seems fitted to throw some light on the problem and give some direction to the scientific treatment of it. That is the assertion that, in a socialistic state, nothing of the nature of interest on capital would exist. To disprove this proposition, or, better, to find the necessary and sufficient conditions under which the socialistic state could dispense with interest on capital altogether, is a task which forces us to a careful investigation into some of the deepest and most interesting questions concerning the demand side of the capital-market. For this purpose we need first of all to know what is meant by a "socialistic state" and in what manner this state would calculate the prices of the different commodities. To have cleared up ideas on this fundamental point is the merit, not of *William Thompson* and *Marx*, but of *Robert Owen* and *Rodbertus*.[1]

The theory of interest was at the same time diverted to another unfruitful line of highly hypothetical controversy, namely the discussion of what is commonly known as the *Wages Fund Theory*. To every one accustomed to think on economic questions, it is plain enough that general progress, specially the growth of population and the rise in the standard of life of the working classes, must in some measure depend upon the supply of capital. The advocates of the Wages Fund Theory treated the explanation of this connection very lightly : the function of Capital was to serve as a " Subsistence Fund," advanced to the labouring class. The amount of this fund was fixed irrespective of the demand. And the demand was simply the arithmetical product of the number of labourers and the average of their earnings. Thus, as soon as one of these factors is supposed to be constant, every in-

---

[1] Comp. *Cassel*: " Das Recht auf den vollen Arbeitsertrag. Eine Einführung in die theoretische Oekonomie."

crease in the other is strictly limited by the supply of capital.

Among the innumerable *à priori* assumptions upon which the Wages Fund Theory was built, we have here only to point out those which seem to be of special importance for the theory of interest. Supposing a society to have a definite sum to advance in the form of wages, and supposing also the number of the population given, it does not follow from that that anything is known as to the standard of wages. The theory implied however two other assumptions which were not expressly stated ; namely 1st, that *the period of advances was the same* in all branches of production ; 2nd, that this period was *constant* and equal to one year, the period of production in agriculture. But if we suppose a certain capital advanced as wages to a certain number of labourers *for one year*, then of course the yearly wage of a single labourer is determined by a simple division ; while, so long as no assumption is made as to the length of the period of advance, the yearly wages of the single labourer remain undetermined.

The first of these assumptions is an outcome of the vicious habit of reasoning on *averages* and means, where we should, and very well could, go to the *actual facts* So long as this custom prevails—and it prevails still in our science to a very great extent —we cannot expect to understand phenomena which are the very effects of the variety and *non-uniformity* of real economic life. And, more particularly, so long as we continue to substitute an average period of investment for the really infinite variety of such periods in different branches of production, we cannot hope to detect the influence which a fall in the rate of interest has in directing the general demand for commodities (and therefore social production), preponderantly towards such commodities as require comparatively a greater amount of that productive agent named " Use of Capital." The second of the assumptions referred to, viz. that the average period of advance is *constant*, seems to have had for a long time all the force of a tradition, in hindering economists from seeing that the period of advance which is most economical at any particular rate of interest necessarily *varies* with that rate. And it was not till the genius of *Jevons* definitely broke with the old tradition, that economists began to appreciate the bearing of this truth on the theory of interest.

Equally unfruitful was the Wages Fund Theory in investigating the forces which govern the *supply* of Capital. Its advocates adopted the *Smith-Ricardian* formula that accumulation would ultimately be checked by a continuous fall in the rate of interest ; but they gave this statement a much more absolute meaning than it had had before. They held that every attempt of the labourers to extract higher wages must necessarily lead to a fall in the rate of interest and this to a decrease of accumulation and of the sum total advanced as wages ; so that the wages would again be reduced at least to their old level. This highly hypothetical reasoning contains, among others, the supposition that *every* fall in the current rate of interest would weaken the inducement to save, and thus diminish the supply of Capital. But though the whole Wages Fund Theory essentially depended on this supposition, it does not appear that the advocates of the theory ever troubled themselves with serious investigation' into the connections between the variations of interest and the accumulation of Capital. These connections therefore still remain to be examined before we can have a complete theory of interest.

Thus the Wages Fund Theory in many different respects worked as a check on the development of the theory of interest. Through adapting the results of their extremely abstract and hypothetical reasoning immediately to the questions of actual life, the supporters of the theory did much to mislead economic and social policy; but it may be doubted whether they did not do still greater harm to economic theory, by discrediting it, for generations to come, in the eyes of all practical men. And the theory of interest has probably not suffered least through this general contempt for theoretical investigations.

§ 6. *For What is Interest Paid?* I. *The Supply Side.*

At the same time that these barren speculations prevailed, there was already some beginning of the analytic work which was to be the positive contribution of the nineteenth century to the theory of interest. This work may be said to have concentrated itself on the question :—For what is interest paid? But the object of a bargain may always be looked upon from two different points of view : that of the seller and that of the buyer. We may ask, what is it that the seller gives? and we may ask, what is it that the buyer receives? Thus in the case of interest the object of the bargain very naturally presented itself under two different aspects : Some economists laid stress upon the analysis of the sacrifice for which the lender is compensated; while others confined their attention rather to the advantage for which the borrower paid. It is convenient to follow the development of the theory according to this division of the subject. But we should always bear in mind that we have to deal here with two different sides of one and the same thing, and that an author who emphasises one side is not therefore to be supposed ignorant of the other.

Let us begin, then, with the supply side. *Senior*, seeking to analyse the " Instruments of Production," divided them into three groups : " Labour," " Natural Agents," and " Abstinence." " Although Human Labour and the Agency of Nature independently of that of man, are the Primary Productive Powers, they require the concurrence of a Third Productive Principle to give to them complete efficiency. The most laborious population, inhabiting the most fertile territory, if they devoted all their labour to the production of immediate results, and consumed its produce as it arose, would soon find their utmost exertions insufficient to produce even the mere necessaries of existence. To the Third Principle or Instrument of Production, without which the two others are inefficient, we shall give the name of *Abstinence*." Having thus placed Abstinence, as a necessary factor of production, on the same line as the other factors, *Senior* had to explain why Abstinence was scarce, so scarce that it must be paid for. " To abstain from the enjoyment which is in our power, or to seek distant rather than immediate results, are among the most painful exertions of the human will . . . of all the means by which man can be raised in the scale of being, abstinence, as it is perhaps the most effective, is the slowest in its increase, and the least generally diffused." [1]

To this clear statement *Senior* need only have added, in order to escape misapprehension, that interest is determined by the price which must be offered for the *marginal* abstinence ; or that, though a certain quantity of abstinence may very well be had at a lower price and perhaps for less than nothing, a higher price must be paid, indifferently to *all* abstinence, in order to get

[1] *Senior N. W.*: Outlines of the Science of Political Economy, 5th Ed. pp. 58–60.

the *sufficient* quantity, *i.e.* a quantity which will satisfy the demand on the market. This, however, he omitted to do, and thus it became an easy task for *Lassalle* to make the whole conception of "abstinence" ridiculous by representing the millionaires of Europe, the Rothschilds, etc. as ascetics for the sake of society.[1] The very word Abstinence seems to assume an element of moral merit, and this makes it unsuitable to be used in an objective analysis, where it is an essential condition that the *what is* should be strictly separated from the *what ought to be*. The confusion between these two questions has always proved to be exceedingly detrimental to the theory of interest, and for this reason it is after all not to be deplored that the term "Abstinence" became discredited and ultimately dropped out of use.[2]

In France, *Bastiat*, though certainly not a very strong thinker, made some valuable remarks on the special question which now occupies us, and showed himself very apt at finding good expressions for the function of the lender. "To save is deliberately to put an interval between the moment when the services are made for the society, and that when the equivalent is received from it." This *ajournement* is the object of exchange and the price of it is interest. The reason why this service is scarce

[1] *Lassalle,* "Herr Bastiat-Schultze von Delitzsch, der oekon. Julian, oder: Kapital und Arbeit." Berlin 1864.

[2] *Senior* himself was not quite satisfied with his term: "We are aware that we employ the word Abstinence in a more extensive sense than is warranted by common usage." He regarded abstinence not only as a productive service, but also as a factor, in the process by which prices are determined, in every respect on the same line with "labour" and the "agency of nature": "By the word Abstinence, we wish to express that agent, distinct from labour and the agency of nature, the concurrence of which is necessary to the existence of Capital, and which stands in the same relation to Profit as Labour does to Wages." (loc. cit. p. 59.)

is given in the same manner as by *Senior:* In order to resolve to accumulate Capital, a man must indeed provide for the future and sacrifice the present for it.[1]

Cairnes accepted *Senior's* term " Abstinence " ; but he adopted also the new, and probably the better term, *postponement.* He regarded this as a *sacrifice,* the one of his two great groups of sacrifices, labour being the other.   He even observed that, whilst postponement is no proper sacrifice for the rich, still it "will frequently demand the most rigorous self-denial" on the part of the poor.   But, instead of drawing from this statement the natural conclusion that interest must be high enough to pay for the *marginal* postponement, he attempts to bring it into accordance with the *à priori* and entirely arbitrary formula with which he starts : "Cost means sacrifice."   He tells us not to look upon "what is personal and peculiar" ; "the sacrifices to be taken account of, and which govern exchange value, are, not those undergone by A, B, or C, but the *average* sacrifices undergone by the class of labourers or capitalists to which the producers of the commodity belong."   This is false in substance, and seems moreover to reduce the doctrine of sacrifice, as the measure of cost of production, to

---

[1] *Bastiat,* Harmonies Economiques 2 Ed. Paris 1851. The following quotation gives a good idea of *Bastiat's* views and at the same time of his vivid style. A business man addresses a money-lender thus : "Vous avez droit à recevoir immédiatement une valeur, et il vous convient de ne la recevoir que dans dix ans. Eh bien ! pendant ces dix ans substituez-moi à votre droit, mettez-moi à votre lieu et place. Je toucherai pour vous la valeur dont vous êtes créancier ; je l'emploierai pendant dix ans sous une forme productive, et vous la restituerai à l'échéance. Par là vous me rendrez un *service* et comme tout service a une valeur, qui s'apprécie en la comparant à un autre service, il ne reste plus qu'à estimer celui que je sollicite de vous, à en fixer *la valeur.*" [Ch. XV. *De l'épargne,* p. 419.]

something still more arbitrary and incomprehensible.[1]

Cairnes had observed that the *measure of abstinence* was quantity of wealth into duration of abstinence. To this *Macvane* makes some objections which seem to be essentially wrong ; and as the question of the measure or dimension of abstinence is of the highest importance for a clear conception of this service, his reasoning seems to deserve a closer analysis. He says : " Now, the quantity of wealth abstained from is gauged by its value ; and its value depends on its cost of production. If, then, we introduce abstinence as an element in determining value, and value as a factor in the measure of abstinence, we are clearly guilty of using the thing to be measured as part and parcel of our standard for measuring it."— " Abstinence is not itself a primary fact of industry . . . the more fundamental fact is the length of time that must elapse between the outlay of labour and the possession of the finished product."[2] *Macvane* therefore proposes to replace the term abstinence by the term *Waiting*. By this he seems to mean that "waiting" does not contain more than one element—is a "quantity of one dimension," the dimension of time. This is, of course, inadmissible ; " waiting a certain time " means nothing, when it is not stated *what* is postponed. Perhaps it is *Macvane's* intention that "waiting" should be taken to denote postponement of some *concrete* thing or enjoyment. But in that case we should have to give up the character of waiting as an arithmetical quantity, and this would make waiting a very useless conception. But there is a still graver

---

[1] *Cairnes*, Some Leading Principles of Political Economy newly expounded ; London 1874 (pp. 88–95 and p 60).

[2] Quarterly Journal of Economics (Harvard University) Vol. I.; Boston 1887. *Macvane*, Analysis of Cost of Production.

objection to such a definition of waiting.   There *is* very seldom a postponement of anything concrete ; the man who saves does not as a rule know what he would have used his money for, if he had not saved it ; he simply postpones the consumption of a certain sum of *value.*   Hence "waiting" is, *as a matter of fact,* measured by the product of such a sum of value and the time of waiting.   This measure gives the ultimate definition of waiting ; and waiting in this sense is one of the services which constitute the concrete costs of production.   It seems to have been the aim of *Macvane* to find these costs as distinguished from their values or from what *Marshall* calls "expenses of production."[1]   It is interesting to observe how impossible it is, even if we go back to these very elements of the process by which prices are fixed, to dispense with the element of price itself.   This seems to be a horror to *Macvane* as well as to so many other economists. But, after all, why should we trouble ourselves about this difficulty any more than a mathematician does, when he assumes the unknowns of his problem to be known and works with them until he arrives at that system of equations which ultimately determines them ?

The term *waiting* has been accepted by *Marshall* as equivalent to "postponement of enjoyment" ;[2] and thus we may perhaps assume the term to be definitely established in economic science, at least so far as the Teutonic languages are concerned. To the French it seems most natural to adopt the term "*ajournement*" already used by *Bastiat.*   Both terms signify the same, viz. the service of the lender, as measured by the product of the value postponed

---

[1] *Marshall,* Principles of Economics, Vol. I. 4th ed. Book V. Ch. III. § 2.

[2] Ibid.   Book IV. Ch. VII. § 8 ; and Book VI. Ch. VI. § 3.

and the time of waiting. Hence the analysis of the question, "for what is interest paid?" might be said to have reached a definite result as far as the supply side of the capital market is concerned.

But much work remains to be done before we get a real knowledge of the manner in which the total amount of waiting depends on the rate of interest. As to such knowledge, we cannot pride ourselves on being much in advance of the English authors of the seventeenth century, such as *Sir Josiah Child* and *Sir William Petty*.[1] Writers who have entered upon the question have mostly confined themselves to remarks on the general under-estimation of future goods as compared with present, and the consequent necessity of paying interest in order to call forth a certain quantity of waiting.[2] Thus *Karl Menger* observes that the condition for enjoying the advantages of capitalistic production is the willingness to provide for longer periods, and proceeds to show

[1] Comp. above p. 10 n. 4 and p. 11 etc.

[2] Among the earlier writers on this subject *John Rae* should specially be mentioned as having made the most valuable observations on the circumstances influencing people's desire to save. [New Principles of Political Economy, Boston 1834.] The best of these were quoted by *John Stuart Mill* (Principles of Political Economy, Book I. Ch. XI.) and thus made familiar to economists. But *Rae's* general theory of interest is a failure, owing mainly to his assumption that the desire of accumulation in any society may be expressed simply by the rate of interest at which people are willing to save, or, as he puts it in his somewhat strange terms, "by the length of the period, to which the inclination of its members to yield up a present good, for the purpose of producing the double of it at the expiration of that period, will extend." [*Rae*, Book II. Ch. VI.] Of course there is, *at every rate of interest*, some desire to save; what the actual rate will be, is determined by the demand for the use of Capital; hence the rate may vary considerably solely on the ground that demand varies. Mathematically, the total amount of waiting supplied in any society may be regarded as a function of the rate of interest. The desire of accumulation is then characterised by the general form of this function and by its constants, but not by the independent variable, the rate of interest.

that this willingness is limited by circumstances connected with the very nature of human life and mind. So far as the necessities of life (and indeed even those of efficiency) are concerned, the satisfaction of present wants must come first as a *sine qua non*. And, according to all that we know about the human mind, a present enjoyment is, as a rule, preferred to a future one of the same intensity.[1]

The underestimation of future goods as compared with present is, however, no new discovery. It has been familiar to most writers who have contributed to the progress of the theory of interest, though it has been expressed by them in different ways.[2] What *Menger* proves is in fact merely that waiting, under certain economic conditions, must be a *sacrifice*. This statement does not, however, tell us very much. What

[1] *Menger*, Grundsätze der Volkswirtschaftslehre, Wien 1871. "Die wirtschaftenden Menschen können . . . dadurch, dass sie die occupatorische Wirtschaft verlassen und zur Heranziehung von Gütern der höheren Ordnungen zur Befriedigung ihrer Bedürfnisse fortschreiten, allerdings die ihnen verfügbaren Genussmittel nach Massgabe dieses ihres Fortschrittes vermehren, aber nur mit der Beschränkung dass sie in demselben Masse, als sie zu Gütern höherer Ordnung fortschreiten, die Zeiträume hinausrücken, auf welche sich ihre vorsorgliche Thätigkeit erstreckt."—" In diesem Umstande liegt nun aber eine wichtige Schranke des wirtschaftlichen Fortschrittes. Auf die Sicherstellung der den Menschen zur Erhaltung ihres Lebens und ihrer Wohlfahrt in der Gegenwart, oder der nächsten Zukunft erforderlichen Genussmittel ist stets ihre ängstlichste Sorge gerichtet, eine Sorge, die sich in dem Grade abschwächt, je ferner der Zeitraum ist, auf welchem sie sich erstreckt. Diese Erscheinung ist keine Zufällige, sondern im Wesen der menschlichen Natur tief begründet. Soweit nämlich von der Befriedigung unserer Bedürfnisse die Erhaltung unseres Lebens abhängig ist, muss die Sicherstellung der Befriedigung der Bedürfnisse früherer Zeiträume notwendiger Weise jener der spätern vorangehen " . . . Auch "ein Genuss pflegt den Menschen, wie alle Erfahrung lehrt, in der Gegenwart, oder in einer nähern Zukunft wichtiger zu erscheinen, als ein solcher von gleicher Intensität in einem entfernteren Zeitpuncte." (p. 127.)

[2] *Mill* expressly tells us that in China "a much lower estimate of the future relatively to the present " prevails (than in Europe). Book I. Ch. XI. § 3.

we want to know is how far such circumstances prevail in actual life ; to what extent interest must be
paid to balance the sacrifice of waiting ; in one word,
we must find *quantitative* relations between the rate
of interest and the total amount of waiting supplied.

§ 7. II. *The Demand Side.   (a) Use of Capital; its
identity with Waiting.*

The most natural expression for the service received by the borrower is "*use of capital.*"   But
this term is in itself vague and leads to the question:
In what consists the use of capital?   We have seen
how *Turgot* reduced the analysis of this use to its
very elements : the use of a certain quantity of value
during a certain time.   What we find now is a whole
succession of German writers, in the middle part of
the nineteenth century, entering on the problem
without, as it seems, having appreciated the bearing
and importance of *Turgot's* analysis.

This school, of which *Hermann* is one of the first
and most prominent representatives, starts from the
consideration of a concrete use of a concrete capital.
Such use is, of course, possible only in the case of a
durable commodity—one which is not consumed
when used.   The typical case which these writers
had in their minds was therefore that of absolute
durability ; the case of a commodity which can be
used continually without being destroyed. *Hermann*,
in accordance with this view, puts "capital" on the
same line with "land."

Such uses obtain on the market a certain price,
and this price is interest. *Hermann*, who seems to
have studied *Say* with care, gives a good exposition
of the mechanism of the market, and explains how
interest depends on the scarcity of certain uses of
capital.   This is not only correct, but is of some

value, because it gives to the principle of scarcity the prominent place that it deserves. But it is no ultimate explanation of interest. All we learn is that, by the action of supply and demand, prices are fixed on the market, for the use of a certain durable article as well as for that article itself. The proximate cause determining the price of the article is of course its cost of production ; the proximate causes governing the price of the use are the demand for that use and its actual scarcity. But we are never told what relations exist between the demand for the use and the demand for the commodity itself, or between the price of the former and the price of the latter, *i.e.* between interest and capital-value. What we ultimately want to know, however, is just the causes governing the proportion between the sum paid as interest and the value of the capital, *i.e.* the *rate* of interest. Thus there is an essential defect in this whole analysis of interest.

The nature of this defect becomes clearer if we proceed as we have just done and consider only the use of absolutely durable commodities. But the representatives of the Use-school could not of course confine their investigations to this limited field. They had to extend their conception of "use" to cover all cases in which interest is paid. This they did by means of a series of highly artificial cases. There are some goods which possess a practically infinite durability, where only current repairs are provided for. A well-built house is a good instance. When let under the condition that the occupier shall provide for necessary repairs, it affords a good example of an everlasting capital for the use of which pure interest is paid. From this it was but a step to go on to cases where, *e.g.* a machine is gradually worn out in the course of its use, and where, out of the price received for the products, a fund is gradually set aside to provide a new machine.

In such cases we may imagine that there is a capital lasting for ever, but continually changing its material form. And, eventually, there is nothing to hinder us from extending this even to the case where the commodity, as, for instance, coal, is consumed at once by a single use : the capital, coal, is indeed transformed into a capital of another form, but the capital continues to exist and is quantitatively unaltered.

The reader will see how, under these artificial extensions of the original proposition, the very conception of " use of capital " is gradually transformed, becomes more and more abstract, and ends in being nothing more than a " disposition over quantities of capital-goods during certain spaces of time." This also was the point at which the Use-school ultimately arrived, the quoted formula being that accepted by the writer in whom the whole school may be said to have culminated, *Karl Menger*. And thus the development ended in the same result as had been obtained by *Turgot* more than a century before, when he declared the use of capital to be " the use of a certain quantity of value during a certain time." In this conception we have the Use of Capital isolated as a true element of production ; and from this point every further explanation of the *rôle* of capital will have to start. Especially should it be observed that the part which capital plays in the concrete use of a durable article is to be explained from its general function, and not inversely as the Use-school tried to do.

It seems as if even a superficial observer would be able to discover that the advantage which can be derived from the disposition over a certain quantity of value during a certain time is of two different kinds ; that there are two essentially different causes which make such disposition necessary, viz. that *production* needs time and that *consumption* of durable goods needs time. Yet very little attention seems to have been paid to this fundamental distinction.   There are some technical characteristics of production which make it necessary, or at least advantageous, that a certain time should elapse between some of the acts of production and the obtaining of the final product.   Therefore *production* needs use of capital.   But, on the other hand, some forms of consumption are of such a nature that it is technically impossible to get the whole use-value at once out of a produced machine or commodity ; hence such forms of *consumption* necessitate a certain quantity of waiting.

Writers who have tried to carry the analysis of the use of capital a step further, have generally confined their investigations, in a very one-sided manner, to the first part of this distinction.   That use of capital which enables us to put an interval between effort and result in production has, therefore, been studied pretty thoroughly ; but the bearing of this function of capital on the explanation of interest has been exaggerated.

The analysis of the conception "use of capital" would not be complete unless it ended in a definition of the use of capital as an arithmetical quantity. The formula adopted by *Turgot* and re-affirmed by *Menger*, however, is just such a definition : it follows immediately from it that the use of capital is a quantity of two dimensions, the measure of it being a certain sum of value into the time of use.   Now, this is the same measure as that of waiting ; and consequently we may infer that Waiting and Use of Capital denote the *same thing*.   In fact, they signify one and the same productive service : "waiting" is used to express what is done by him who supplies the service, and "use of capital" to express what is obtained by him who buys the service.[1]

[1] This identity of the two conceptions was certainly recognised by *Jevons*, who used in reference to them the terms, "abstinence"

The recognition of the essential unity between waiting and use of capital is, more than anything else, calculated to do away, once and for all, with that dualism in the explanation of interest which indeed was always to be found in one-sided writers of inferior rank but has been so pre-eminently emphasised by recent criticism.

§ 8. *The Demand Side ; (b) Productivity of the Use of Capital.*

When we see a machine automatically making screws it is natural enough to say that the machine produces the screws, just as we say that the labourer produces the hand-made screws. If we now, for the sake of simplicity, suppose such a machine to last for ever, we may say that the product represents the interest on the machine, this being itself regarded as a concrete piece of capital. Hence we might conclude that the capital *produces* the interest. We should then have what might be called a "*productivity theory of interest.*" There have always

and "amount of investment." He gave, however, different expressions for their dimensions. The dimension of capital (i.e. of value of commodity) being M, that of time T, *Jevons* found the dimension of investment to be MT. But for the dimension of abstinence he put UT, U being the dimension of "final degree of utility." It does not seem, however, correct to use such a term : it cannot be anything but fictitious, so long as we have not really established a method of directly measuring intensities of feeling. The only measure of utility available for the economist seems to be the *price* offered for the commodity ; and, if we accept this measure, we must replace U by M in the dimension for abstinence given by *Jevons*. This dimension becomes then identical with that of investment of capital.—The objections to representing "utility" as an arithmetical quantity are given with more detail in "Grundriss einer elementaren Preislehre" by *G. Cassel.* (Zeitschrift für die gesamte Staatswissenschaft, Tübingen, 1899).

been writers who emphasised this side of the function of capital in production.   But such a writer should not, for that reason, be supposed to be ignorant of the fact that all prices, including interest, are regulated, ultimately, by supply and demand.

Lord Lauderdale may be taken as a representative of this group of writers.   He tells us, "that in every instance where capital is so employed as to produce a profit, it uniformly arises, either from its supplanting a portion of labour, which would otherwise be performed by the hand of man ; or from its performing a portion of labour, which is beyond the reach of the personal exertion of man to accomplish."   This statement is not only in the main correct, but contains also in its second part an important truth which has been far too often overlooked by later writers.   In accordance with this view, *Lauderdale* calls capital "productive." But he knows very well that the prices of its services are regulated, like all other prices, by supply and demand.   "The actual profit drawn for the use of any machine when universally adopted, must be regulated on the same principle with the hire of a field, or the payment of an artist, or the price of any other commodity ; that is, the proportion betwixt the quantity of machines that can be easily procured, and the demand for them."[1]

There is not much to be said *against* this analysis.[2] But it is not complete.   It stops just where the more special explanation of interest should begin. The meaning is evidently that there is a market for the productive services of machines and of other concrete forms of capital as well as for these concrete

[1] *Lauderdale*, An Inquiry into the Nature and Origin of Public Wealth.   Edinburgh 1804, pp. 161 and 167.

[2] Expressly to deny the productivity of capital seems only to make the theory of interest more paradoxical and strange to practical men than it ought to be.

time is spent on it, each subsequent extension of time will cause a smaller increase of the produce than before.

Now, as the producer has to pay interest for his use of capital, he cannot extend the time of production indefinitely. He is bound by the condition that the productivity of the *marginal* extension shall never go below what he has to pay for that extension in the form of interest. Hence he must stop at the point where the increase of the product is just swallowed up by the extra interest he has to pay. For every further increase of the time of production will, according to *Jevons'* general assumption, cause a still smaller increase of the produce. Consequently, when interest is high, such methods of production must be adopted as require relatively less time ; while a low rate of interest permits the producer to adopt longer and technically more efficient processes. Thus it is seen that the time which will be spent in the production of any commodity, is one of the *variables* in the problem of interest, and cannot for this reason be assumed.

This deep analysis of the demand side of the capital market is *Jevons'* contribution to the theory of interest. But the chief statements in which he formulated his views were not quite accurate. It is not quite correct to say that the only use of capital is to enable the producer to put an interval between beginning and end of a production process. For as we have seen above, capital, or better waiting, may also be used to give time for the gradual consumption of a durable commodity. Further, it is not true that the sole use of more capital, even in the form of consumable goods, is to make the time of production longer : an increase of capital may just as well be used for an extension of the total volume of production, without any alteration of the production process or of the time it needs. Hence it cannot be correct to represent the productivity of capital as a function of the time alone ; it is just as much a function of the quantity of capital used.[1]

Everybody knows that interest is paid in proportion to the capital lent and in proportion to the duration of the loan, *i.e.* in proportion to the product of value and of time. Hence it is clear *à priori* that value and time must be symmetrical quantities in the theory of interest. A producer who pays for a certain quantity of waiting may use it in two different ways : he may enlarge his whole business without altering his methods, and thus use more capital ; or he may adopt new and more roundabout processes, and thus use more time. In both cases he is limited by the condition that the productivity of the last increment of "the use of capital" shall be great enough to counterbalance the interest paid for that increment. Hence interest is governed by the marginal productivity of the quantity of capital as well as by the marginal productivity of the extension of the time of production.[2]

A theory which has to explain why and in what manner production needs capital should not so emphasise one use of it as to overlook the other ; if it does so, it will often find itself incapable of explaining, within its own sphere, simple events of actual life. Let us, in order to clear our thoughts by a concrete example, imagine a people in a primitive

---

[1] This is evident enough if we consider that waiting, or use of capital, is necessarily a quantity of two dimensions, the measure of it being "quantity of value × time," *i.e.* MT. The effect of this service must, therefore, be a function of m and t and not of t alone.

[2] *Jevons* regarded the productivity as a function of t alone ; as a matter of fact it is a function of t and m and should be denoted by F (m, t). Interest is governed by the differential quotient $\dfrac{\delta F}{\delta m}$ just as well as by $\dfrac{\delta F}{\delta t}$.

stage of agriculture, where tools and machines are simple and few, and the capital of the country consists mainly of the annual harvest. In a good year this capital will be increased, and the increment will be used, not for an extension of the period of production, which remains constant and equal to one year, but for an extended cultivation of land. Probably "the principle of diminishing returns" will come into force, and the rate of interest will then be regulated by the marginal productivity of the capital used in such extension of agriculture. A theory, then, which maintained that interest is governed, in all cases, by the productivity of the last increment of the period of production would not be able to give any explanation of such fluctuations of the rate of interest ; at any rate the explanation would be very formal and not tell us much about the actual connection between causes and effects. Similarly such a theory would fail to explain a rise of interest caused by a simple increase of the population, supposing agricultural land of the same quality as that formerly cultivated to be abundant. Or, to go to the actual facts of our own age, such a theory would give us a very inadequate idea of all those fluctuations of interest, or differences in the rate of interest between different countries, which depend on differences in the rate of the growth of population or similar causes.

§ 9. *Böhm-Bawerk and the Theory of Interest.*

We have seen how, even by the seventeenth century, the problem of interest began to be treated as a problem of supply and demand, and how the foundation of a scientific theory of interest was thus laid. We have seen also how the mechanism of the market on which interest is determined was studied with considerable success by writers of the eighteenth century, particularly by *Turgot* and *Say ;* how the nineteenth century brought a long series of investigations into special questions relating to the supply side or to the demand side of this market ; that the study of particular details did not involve a complete overlooking of other details, nor of the general connections between them ; but that many of the writers to whom we owe valuable contributions to these investigations inclined to regard as the whole theory that which was in fact only the explanation of a special point in it. Thus although much important work was done, scarcely anyone had understood how to make the full use of it, *i.e.* to give every particular truth its organic place in a systematic theory of interest.

Such was the situation when the Austrian economist *Böhm-Bawerk* set himself to write on broad lines a history of the theory of interest and afterwards a positive theory of his own. The general drift of the critical part of this work may be described in a few words. *Böhm-Bawerk* throughout represents as an independent theory that which is in reality only an explanation of a special part of the problem of interest—and indeed is very often clearly stated as such by the writers in question. Thus he succeeds easily enough in proving that this so-called theory fails to give a definite solution of the problem. In this manner he is able to dispose of the majority of his predecessors. But there are, as we have seen, some writers who have had a more comprehensive view of the problem, and have therefore entered upon more than one of the special sides of the theory. These writers are, in *Böhm-Bawerk's* view, only inconsistent. He who holds two different theories at once, cannot, of course, be anything but illogical. Hence it follows that precisely those writers who have done most for the development of a systematic theory of interest, are represented by *Böhm-Bawerk* as eclectics, picking up pieces of every theory just as it may be convenient, but incapable of consistent thought. *Say* is full of contradictions, because he thinks that the use that can be made of capital in production is a factor determining interest just as much as the scarcity of the services of the saver. *Malthus* is classified as an advocate of the " productivity theory," though he has pointed out clearly enough that interest depends just as much on the scarcity of capital as on its productivity ; *Böhm-Bawerk* thinks the remarks relating to the scarcity "*too lightly sounded to drown*" those relating to the productivity ! *Adam Smith* is of course not less guilty of contradictions,[1] and *Samuel Read*, who wrote in 1829 to defend the old theory of demand and supply against *Ricardo's* theory of labour as the standard of value, and who took a comprehensive view of the factors determining interest on both sides of the market, is classified as an eclectic.[2] In this group we find also, among English writers, *John Stuart Mill* and *Jevons*, among German, *Roscher*. It may be admitted that the essential merits of *Roscher* did not lie in strong and systematic thinking, but it seems hard that he should be accused of inconsistency and contradiction on the ground that, having observed that "the price paid for the use of capital naturally depends on the relation between supply and demand, especially of circulating capital," he should think himself obliged to give some reasons why neither supply nor demand would permit the rate of interest to sink to nil. "The legitimateness of interest," he tells us, "is based on two unquestionable grounds :

[1] Comp. above p. 23.
[2] *Read*, Political Economy ; an Inquiry into the natural grounds of right to vendible property or wealth. Edinburgh 1829.

on the real productiveness of capital and on the real abstinence from enjoyment of it by one's self." A decline of the rate of interest is checked, for example, in the first instance, by "every extension of the limits of productive land ;" in the second instance, by the fact that "there are numberless persons who would rather consume their capital, or invest it in hazardous speculations than put it out at interest at 1 per cent. a year."[1] These very sensible remarks show how much indeed *Roscher* had learned from the history of the theory ; and *Böhm-Bawerk's* treatment of him affords a rather typical instance of how incorrect and misleading his criticism generally is.

The weakness of this criticism is, however, itself a fact for which we must seek some plausible explanation. Why should so diligent an investigator, with such very extensive knowledge of the literature, be unable to trace even the main lines of the development of the theory of interest, or to recognise what the individual writers have contributed to its organic growth ? Why should he so often fail to understand even the general position of the authors whom he undertakes to criticise ?

The key to this question, and at the same time to *Böhm-Bawerk's* positive theory of interest, seems to lie in his view of value. The following words, with which he begins his review of *Menger*, throw a strong light on his whole position :

" The superiority of *Menger* to all his predecessors consists in this, that he builds his interest

---

[1] *Roscher*, Principles of Political Economy, transl. from the 13th (1877) German edition, by *Lalor ;* Vol. II. New York 1878. Sec. 188 and 189. " A loan which pays no interest is a donated use of capital. Interest may be called the reward of abstinence " . . . is a passage characteristic of *Roscher's* comprehensive view of the subject.

theory on a much more complete theory of value,—
a theory which gives an elaborate and satisfactory
answer to the very difficult question of the relation
between the value of products and that of their
means of production. Does the value of a product
depend on the value of its means of production, or
does the value of the means of production depend
on that of their products? As regards this question
economists up till *Menger's* time had been very much
groping in the dark. It is true that a number of
writers had occasionally used expressions to the
effect that the value of the means of production was
conditioned by the value of their anticipated
product; as, for instance, *Say, Riedel, Hermann,
Roscher.* But these expressions were never put
forward in the form of a general law, and still less
in the form of an adequate logical argument. Moreover, as must have been noticed, expressions are to
be found in these writers which indicate quite the
opposite view; and with this opposite view the great
body of economic literature fully agrees in re-
cognising as a fundamental law that the cost of
goods determines their value.

But so long as economists did not see clearly
on this preliminary question, their treatment of
the interest problem could scarcely be more than
uncertain groping. How could any one possibly
explain in clear outline a difference in value
between two amounts—expenditure of capital and
product of capital—if he did not even know on
which side of the relation to seek for the cause, and
on which side for the effect?

To *Menger*, then, belongs the great merit of
having distinctly answered this preliminary question.
In doing so, he has definitely and for all time in-
dicated the point at which, and the direction in
which, the interest problem is to be solved.

His answer is this: The value of the means

of production is determined always and without exception by the value of their products."[1]

Surely it is not necessary to criticise this. A writer who holds such narrow views on value, who thinks that the chain of cause and effect in economic life can be followed out only in one direction, is necessarily incompetent to sit in judgment on authors who worked on far broader lines.

Even in cases where the idea of mutual dependence was not stated with such conscious clearness as it was by *Turgot* and *J. B. Say*, the general views of the author must very often be supposed to have been in accordance with this fundamental idea. But *Böhm-Bawerk* sets himself in express opposition to it, and must, therefore, to say the least, fail to give a fair representation of the writers he criticises. Indeed, under such circumstances, *Böhm-Bawerk's* whole history of the theory of interest could not fail to be misleading in its general drift and misleading also in almost every detail.

Moreover, if it be true that the problem of interest is one side only of the general problem of prices, and if it be true that supply and demand are variable factors of this problem, mutually governing one another, but ultimately governed by elements belonging partly to the exterior world, partly to the world of human minds, then any one who fails to grasp these fundamental truths must necessarily be incompetent to produce a systematic theory of interest. It cannot be denied that many valuable contributions to the theory of interest are due to writers who have not been quite clear as to the general mechanism of the market, but have worked out some detail of the problem. *Böhm-Bawerk* must, however, be judged from another point of

[1] Capital and Interest; pp 209, 210. Comp. also *Menger*, Grundsätze der Volkswirtschaftslehre, p. 123.

view : he claims to give a *new* and complete theory of interest ; he positively rejects every previous solution of the problem on the ground that it does not give the whole explanation. Hence if he himself fails to give a systematic and complete theory, he has at least failed of his own purpose. The sincere critic, however, will have to go through his work to see if there are not some details which might prove useful as stones wherewith to complete the edifice for which the foundation was laid in the seventeenth century, and which has been building continuously, with more or less success, throughout the two subsequent centuries.

What then is *Böhm-Bawerk's* positive theory of interest ? The central formula by which he claims to give an explanation of the phenomenon of interest is the " *undervaluation of future goods in relation to present.*" This formula is however ambiguous and has, in fact, two different meanings even with *Böhm-Bawerk* himself. First it means the same thing as earlier writers intended to express when they accentuated the fact that abstinence means sacrifice ; and there are instances when this thought was formulated in very much the same words as those used by *Böhm-Bawerk*. Thus *Bastiat* says : " In order to decide to accumulate a capital you must provide for the future and sacrifice the present for it." And we have seen how *Menger* formulated the same idea in the words : a present enjoyment is, as a rule, preferred to a future one of the same intensity (p. 44).

Nor does *Böhm-Bawerk* seem to have added much to the analysis of the real conditions of waiting, or to our knowledge of the effects of variations in the rate of interest upon the quantity of waiting offered. Yet, as we have already seen, it was just at this point that a further investigation into actual facts was most urgently needed.

But the " undervaluation of future goods " is also taken by *Böhm-Bawerk* to mean the final result of all the forces acting on the market.   The " under-valuation " in this more general sense is however no *explanation* of the phenomenon of interest.   The mere fact that interest is paid shows that present goods have a higher " social value " than future ones.   To give the grounds for the existence of interest is therefore quite the same as to explain why future goods have a lower value.   Thus *Böhm-Bawerk's* great formula turns out to be nothing more than a scheme by which the theory of interest *can* be worked out.   We may say that " *interest is an agio obtained by present goods in exhange for future ones ;* " the problem then is to study the forces acting on both sides of this exchange.   This manner of stating the problem of interest, which has been announced and even believed in as a great discovery, is how-ever neither new nor profitable.   We have found the same idea in the comparison between interest and agio in exchange, which was usual in the seventeenth century.[1]   And *Bentham* writes : " Those who have the resolution to sacrifice the present to future, are natural objects of envy to those who have sacrificed the future to the present " ; and in another place he states the whole problem of interest more suggestively in this form : " Putting money out at interest, is exchanging present money for future." [2]

It would of course have been profitable to take up such a formula if it had helped forward the scientific treatment of the problem.   But the very opposite seems to be the case.   If the theory of interest is a side only of the general theory of prices, then, naturally, we must try to give our problem such a form that interest may be said to be a *price* paid for a certain

[1] Comp. above p. 14 n. 2.
[2] *Bentham*, Defence of Usury ; Letter X and Letter II.

object, and this very transaction would therefore be described as a sale or purchase, not as an exchange. Now, the analysis of interest had been, as we have seen, already brought so far long before *Böhm-Bawerk's* time ; it had been stated that interest is a price paid for waiting or—what we have found to be the same—for the use of capital. Hence we must conclude that *Böhm-Bawerk's* formula represents, most distinctly, a step backwards.

His analysis of the reasons for the undervaluation of future goods is also, as we might expect, very insufficient. He gives three such reasons. Of these the first two represent undervaluation in the subjective sense in which we have just used the word ; the third reason is expressed in two ways : present goods are technically superior to future because they help us to produce a *greater quantity* of goods ; and they are superior because this product has a higher *value* than a product obtained by the help of the future goods. The first statement has a meaning only when precisely the same commodities are produced by two processes of different length ; for only under this supposition is a comparison between their quantities possible. But this supposition excludes by far the greater part of the cases where capital is used ; what is produced by more roundabout methods is almost always *other* commodities, or at least commodities of another quality ; and here the products can be compared only through the medium of their prices. The second statement implies a comparison between values, which include an item for interest, *i.e.* just that agio which should be explained. Thus *Böhm-Bawerk* has not isolated the elementary reasons for the existence of the agio as he claims to have done.

Still less has he succeeded in showing how these reasons work together. There is no sharp line of division between the forces which act on the supply side and those which act on the demand side of the capital-market. The lack of a clear grasp of the mechanism of this market is most conspicuous when *Böhm-Bawerk* goes on to speak of the grounds regulating, quantitatively, the rate of interest. These are, curiously enough, not the same as the general grounds for the undervaluation of future goods ; seven new grounds are enumerated, but it is not clear in what relation they stand to the former, nor what position they occupy in the general market.[1]

Particularly incomplete is the analysis of the factors working on the demand side. The single reason given for the use of capital is the technical productivity of an extension of the period of production. Even on this point, on which *Böhm-Bawerk* himself lays so much stress, his work seems not to have advanced our knowledge very much. After a criticism of *Jevons'* theory which can only be characterised as unfair, he makes use of all the essential points in it—even the defects which we have observed above—for his own theory. And he even aggravates some defects of *Jevons'* investigations by emphasising the conception of a "period of production." A precise definition of this very vague idea is of course impossible. We do not know, and can never know, when the latest fruits of our present efforts will ripen. Just as little do we know about the distribution over past centuries of the efforts whose results we now enjoy. Moreover, this last question is quite irrelevant so far as the rate of interest is concerned. Whether it has taken a long or a short time to build a railway or to provide a certain quantity of coal, is of no economic importance, once these things are there. All economic motives lie, at any given moment, in the *future* or the

---

[1] Comp. *Böhm-Bawerk's* criticism of *Malthus ;* Capital and Interest, pp. 151–152.

present ; so do the causes which govern the rate of interest.

"The period of production" might perhaps be made a fruitful conception if there was only *one* period of production in all different branches of industry. But we know that this is not the case, not even approximately ; on the contrary it is one of the most essential points in the theory of interest that different branches of production require very different amounts of "use of capital." Only when we have a clear insight into this fact are we able to understand how alterations in the demand for commodities influence the total quantity of waiting demanded and therefore the rate of interest.[1] Thus it seems much better from all points of view to base the theory of interest directly on our actual knowledge of the amounts of waiting required in different industries and of the variations of these amounts with the rate of interest, rather than to base it on an average which has no correspondence with reality.

The last part of *Böhm-Bawerk's* work seems, however, to indicate some real progress as compared with the writers to whom we have referred above. In it he puts the whole problem on a broader basis and extends his investigations so as to embrace the wages of labour. His conclusion is that there are certain connections between the standard of wages, the rate of interest, and the "length of the period of production" ; this latter is determined by each producer, account being taken of the two other factors, so as to make the whole production as cheap as possible. But owing mainly to the idea that the sole function of capital is to lengthen the period of production, *Böhm-Bawerk's* statement of this important truth is one-sided and, though extremely abstract, not very clear. A student familiar with the "principle of substitu-

---

[1] Comp. above pp. 35–36.

tion " [1] would express it somewhat in the following manner : There are generally in every branch of production some cases where hand-labour or machinery may be used with equal advantage. The use of machinery may, however, as will be explained in detail in the positive part of this book, be resolved into labour (of making it) and waiting. Hence it may be said that in such cases labour and waiting will be substituted for each other in certain proportions. How much shall be used of each of these services depends of course on their prices. If, for instance, wages rise, there will be a certain tendency among employers to use more machinery, *i.e.* to substitute waiting for labour ; the demand for waiting will increase, and its price, the rate of interest, will have a tendency to rise.

All this is nothing more than is within the daily experience of the ordinary business man : by spending a little more capital he is able to reduce his wages bill relatively to the output; only he has then to charge more to the account of interest. Whether he will choose such a course or not will generally in a certain degree depend on the prices of labour and waiting ; but also on other circumstances which in a great many cases have the deciding influence. Economic science cannot, therefore, be satisfied with the *a priori* assumption that the substitution of the use of capital for labour is merely a question of prices ; it is its obvious duty to inquire into the actual conditions of such substitution. Instead of doing this, *Böhm-Bawerk* gives us a series of tables composed of hypothetical figures —a series which proves nothing to the mathematically trained economist, and will probably be found still more wanting by the empirical economist, who above all, looks for facts.

[1] Comp. *Marshall*, Principles of Economics, Book V., Ch. III., § 3.

The principle of substitution evidently affords only one relation between wages, interest, and the demand for labour and capital, and is, therefore, only a subordinate part of a complete explanation of interest. *Böhm-Bawerk* and his followers have endeavoured to build their whole system on this relation, and have, therefore, arrived at a highly artificial theory which has little to do with actual life.

This survey has—if one may presume to say so—corrected some false conceptions with regard to the past history of the theory of interest which have been widely accepted on the authority of *Böhm-Bawerk*. And if the outlines here drawn up truly represent the development of human thought on the subject of interest, they will perhaps prove of some use for further and more detailed historical research. But the principal aim of this chapter has been to state what has been done hitherto for the explanation of interest, and thus to obtain some guidance for answering the question of what remains to be done.

The most important achievement hitherto obtained by the discussion, which has been going on for so many centuries, is that the question, For what is interest paid? may now be regarded as definitely settled. It is stated, once for all, that interest is the price paid for an *independent and elementary factor of production* which may be called either waiting or use of capital, according to the point of view from which it is looked at.

All that remains to be done as regards the theory is, therefore, to explain the causes governing this price; and all discussions of the subject will henceforth have to be based on the general theory of prices. This theory will therefore, first of all, claim our attention.

CHAPTER II

ON PRICES IN GENERAL AND ON INTEREST
CONSIDERED AS A PRICE

§ 1.   *Value and Price.*

"VALUE" is a somewhat vague conception. Writers on economics have from time to time tried to give it a more definite meaning, and several kinds of value have been defined, as, for instance, "value in use" and "value in exchange." But these definitions have generally suffered from a lack of accuracy and precision, and much ambiguity remains as to the meaning to be attached to the word. Consequently a great deal of work has been spent in barren discussions and controversies about the nature of value and the causes governing it.

This could not be otherwise. Whenever "value" means anything else than price, it refers to psychological processes, to intensity of feelings or will. But these forces, though indeed very real, are not capable of objective measurement ; and, therefore, the idea of value will never acquire that arithmetical definiteness so urgently needed for a conception which should serve as the foundation of a science dealing with quantities. It may indeed be said that the vagueness of the term "value" has induced people to speak on general questions of economic theory in a most careless manner; and from the confusion thus caused the science has greatly suffered.

The most radical and effective cure for this evil would of course be to do away with the whole theory of value. Fortunately this is quite possible. There is, in fact, no reason at all why we should commence the study of economics by a separate theory of value. We may with great advantage begin at once with an explanation of *prices* and the general causes governing them. For there is no ambiguity as to what is meant by price. It is familiar to everybody. Price, besides, is in itself a genuine arithmetical conception, such as a quantitative science, like political economy, requires. In fact, money is for every individual a sort of scale by the aid of which he is able to classify his different desires according to their importance, and even in some degree to measure this importance. The measurement may be very imperfect, but still it is that which regulates the economic actions of the individual; and the various desires of the individuals, estimated in money, form in reality the foundation for the settling of prices. It is, therefore, enough for the economist to start from these individual money-estimates, and we need not, as economists, trouble ourselves with the physico-psychological processes which lie behind them.

It should also be observed that "value" is never anything else than a *hypothetical price*, a price that would be agreed upon under certain conditions. For instance, the shopkeeper, announcing that he will sell his stock "below value," thereby wishes to intimate that he will sell below the prices he would have obtained under normal conditions of the market. And the "value-in-use" of the theoretical economist means—where it has any distinct meaning—the highest price that an individual would offer for a commodity, were it not to be had for less. Suppose we take up all conceptions of value in political economy and examine them, we shall invariably find that they mean nothing more than a price that would be reached under certain circumstances ; but as these circumstances are seldom defined with sufficient accuracy, it is no wonder that so much ambiguity prevails about the meaning of the word.

From what has just been said it follows that there can be no reasonable theory of value which is not included in a general theory of prices. And there can be no subject within the scope of political economy which can be better explained by aid of a preliminary study of value than by an inquiry limited to the explanation of prices.

There is, however, one difficulty which deserves to be mentioned in this connection. Here, and throughout what follows, we shall regard money only as a scale for economic estimates. Now, if this scale itself be liable to variations due to the material medium serving as money, the theory of prices cannot be complete without taking notice of these variations. This seems to be one of the reasons why it has been thought necessary to make a separate theory of value : such a theory should explain the relative values of commodities, irrespective of any common measure of value or medium of exchange. But if a theory of money is included, as it ought to be, as an integral part of the general theory of prices, there is no room for objection ; and we have the great advantage of founding our reasoning on clear conceptions and measurable quantities. Accordingly in what follows we shall, to begin with, take our scale of money for granted, and on this assumption try to investigate the nature of interest and the causes governing it. Then we shall have to add a special study of the nature of money and of the influences of variations in the money-scale on the rate of interest. Only when we have done this will it be possible to state the problem of interest in its purest form.

There is another and perhaps still more prominent reason which has caused people to lay stress upon a separate theory of value. Prices are in a certain sense expressions for the *actual* economic conditions of society. But men urgently want to know more than what prices *are* actually paid, or how this or that service *is* remunerated ; they want to know what prices *should* be paid, what is the *right* reward of the different services ; in other words, they want to know the *value* of the different commodities and productive services. Hence the insistence on an independent theory of value. This is specially apparent in Socialist theory. According to the Socialistic school, labour, in the present conditions of society, does not get its just reward ; the working man is wrongly deprived of a part of "the whole produce of his labour." On this ground the Socialists construct a new theory of value which, in fact, is nothing but a theory of prices in an ideal state, where the labourer would get "the whole produce of his labour."

Even in popular language, "value" mostly indicates a price which would be fixed if everything were as it ought to be, *i.e.* in an ideal state of things. "Value" in this sense may therefore shortly be said to denote ideal price.

If we can imagine a society where all prices, those of commodities as well as those of productive services, are fixed in the most just and adequate manner, the study of those prices must tell us everything we want to know about "*social value.*" [By this term we shall understand simply a price in such an ideal state of social economics.] Now every theory of prices must necessarily, in order to simplify the matter, start from some general assumptions as to the prevailing economic conditions ; and it seems very natural to use the ideal conditions as such a starting-point.   If we do this, our general theory of prices will explain everything that would be explained by a separate examination of "social values."

§ 2. *On the ideal system of prices.*

We have seen that the social value of any service rendered to the community means the price that such a service would fetch under an ideal system of price-determination.   Now the question arises : is there any such definite ideal ? and if so, what is it ?   In order to answer this question we have naturally to ask first, why should there be any such thing as price ? what is the purpose of attaching certain prices to commodities and productive services ? is there any necessity for doing so ? or is this custom perhaps merely an outcome of our present social arrangements ?

A few simple remarks will clear up this point. First as to prices put on commodities.   Their purpose and their social function are to regulate the consumption of commodities.   The world is not so rich that every demand can be satisfied.   Hence it is necessary that the demand should in some way be checked and brought into accordance with the supply. This might conceivably be done in the way suggested by the Communists, who propose that the community itself should regulate not only the production but also the individual consumption of its members.   If all members of the community were to eat at the same table, there would of course be no difficulty in regulating the demand ; the community would simply have fixed what everybody should consume.   But if we wish to avoid this extreme regulation and most objectionable interference with our private life, there is no other line open to us but the regulation of demand by means of prices. This method of regulation can, as we all know, be made quite effective, and it has in addition the great advantage of being extremely elastic and of imposing upon the individual the slightest coercion possible.   When we put a certain price on a commodity, we are in fact selecting those individuals whose desire for the commodity is strong enough to induce them to pay this price ; the commodity is offered to them to the exclusion of all others.   This system enables the individual himself to decide to a certain extent on his consumption ; and may be said, in a certain sense, to serve as a selection of the most important needs to be satisfied.

It may be objected that the willingness to pay a certain sum for a commodity depends very much on the power to pay, and does not always indicate the real importance of the need.   But this is an objection against the distribution of income, not against the fixing of the same price for commodities of the same kind.   If the poor cannot satisfy very urgent needs while the rich can satisfy desires of trifling importance, this evil should not be met by selling commodities cheaper to the poor than to the rich, but by increasing in some way the income of the poor.   To offer some commodities or services to the poor under the usual price is practically the same as increasing his income while at the same time compelling him to use it in a certain way.   This may be good policy in some exceptional instances ; but when we are tracing the general drift of economic and social developments we need not take notice of such cases.

We may, on these grounds, regard it as an ideal of social economy that a uniform price should be paid for one and the same item of any commodity.

The principal purpose of this price is to cut off such demand as cannot be satisfied. Hence the reason for a price is always the *scarcity* of the supply. Were the supply so great as to satisfy *every* demand, there would be no reason for a price; and we should not call a thing, supplied in such abundance, a "commodity" or reckon it among "economic goods."

But prices have generally an influence on the supply also. A higher price put on a commodity causes a larger part of the productive services of society to be used in the production of that commodity. Thus a system of prices serves as a regulator, not only of the consumption but also of the whole production of the community. For this purpose it is, however, convenient that the system of prices should be extended to the *factors of production* as well. We must regard as "factors of production" everything that is required in the productive process, and is moreover so scarce, relatively to the total demand for it, that a price must be set on it in order to check the demand. This price must obviously be uniform, so that the same price is paid for the same productive service, whether it be used in one branch of production or in another. If no such uniform price were fixed, there would be no guarantee against the use of the service being pushed further in one line of production than in another and thus against the demand for a special article being satisfied disproportionately, and at the cost of the demand for other articles. Hence we may conclude that a right direction of social production requires uniform prices to be fixed for all productive services as well as for commodities. This holds good even in a socialistic state, which has taken over the whole productive process on its own account; though in this case the fixing of prices, for everything that is not ready for consumption, is merely a matter of bookkeeping.

The fundamental reason why a price should be put on a primary factor of production is the scarcity of that factor. Of many factors, however, the supply may increase if stimulated by a higher price. This is, in some degree, the case with labour and other personal services. Thus price may be regarded as that which must be offered in order to call forth a sufficient amount of such services. But this function of prices is generally only of secondary importance ; and should rather be put somewhat in the background in the first exposition of the theory of prices.

The idea in attaching prices to the factors of production is of course that these prices shall be used in computing the cost of products ; and it is implied in what has been said that the prices of the products should be determined by their cost of production. It is also to be understood that the economy of the society in question is so directed that there is no surplus of articles unsold nor of productive services which cannot find employment.

Thus the consideration of the question, For what purpose are prices needed ? leads us to the conclusion that prices are an indispensable element in social economics. Moreover some general principles for the determination of prices may, as we have seen, be derived from the very *idea* of this process. These principles, which will be referred to in what follows under the name of the " *Cost-principle*," are to be regarded, in an objective sense, as the ideal for every system of prices.[1]

---

[1] It should be observed that there is always some room for what may be called the "Communistic principle." In modern towns, for instance, streets are cleaned and lighted, bridges built, the services of police and firemen supplied, without any special charge being made for the use of such conveniences. The

To every one familiar with the views of the classical school of Free Trade, it is obvious that the ideal system of prices just defined is the same as what this school regarded as the ultimate end of all economic policy. It reflects the greatest credit on the Free-trade-theory to have given us, probably for the first time in the history of economic science, a clear conception of what should be aimed at as the ideal with respect to prices ; and it cannot be doubted that the theory was right on this point. We are only too much inclined to overlook this fact, because we have found that the means by which the Free-traders thought it possible to attain their ideal are quite insufficient for the purpose. We know to-day that what we have called the Cost-principle can never be realised by Free Competition alone. We know that Free Competition is in many cases, impossible, and that the classical assumption of free competition throughout the entire economic society is an illusion. The modern school of social reformers has given economic policy a much broader scope and has taken a great many different social forces into its service. It is, however, interesting to observe that all new lines of economic policy, adopted by the social reformers, which promise anything for the future, tend, so far as prices are concerned, merely to work out the classical ideal of a system of prices. We may in fact say that the first aim of modern social policy is to realise the " social value " of every factor of production, specially, of course, that of labour in

possibility of applying this principle is, however, necessarily in the main confined to objects of *social consumption* such as those just named. And as society always has, in the last instance, to decide whether the usefulness obtained is worth the cost incurred, the Cost-principle is never wholly suspended.—The " Cost-principle " indeed is not quite an adequate term ; but it seems impossible to find a word which will cover the whole of our ideal principles.

all its different degrees. At the same time, there is, no doubt, a much wider scope for social policy ; very much might be done in the way of *increasing* the social value of labour, *e.g.* through education in the broadest sense of the word, through regulating population, etc.

Take for instance the modern Trade-Union-policy. *Sidney and Beatrice Webb*, the leading writers on this subject, have pointed out that the centre of this policy lies in what they call the " Device of the Common Rule." But the aim of that device is obviously to make of all labour of the same kind that uniform market-article postulated by classical economists. And the ideal of a system of prices as regards labour is, according to the authors of " Industrial Democracy," attained, when all labour is organised in open Trade Unions exclusively relying on the policy of the Common Rule.

In a certain sense we may speak of the labourer himself as " produced " and consequently also of the cost of production of labour. It was one of the most disastrous fallacies of the old theory that free competition would be enough to secure to different degrees of labour such wages as would cover the cost of production of that labour. Modern social policy recognises that it is not, and therefore steadily looks out for new methods, such as, *e.g.*, the fixed Minimum Wage, by which to realise the ideal of the Cost-principle as regards the lowest ranks of labour.

And if we look at that special price which is the subject of the present investigation, we shall find that the aim of modern policy in respect to the interest-problem is to realise, as far as possible, a market-rate of interest for every loan, and to prohibit loans of such a character that no market-rate whatever is applicable to them. Thus even in this case the Cost-principle, and more specially the uniformity of prices, may be said to be the central point of the policy adopted.

Association in one form or another between business enterprises is one of the most prominent characteristics of modern economic life. Writers on social policy do not take an altogether adverse attitude towards these combines. They admit that some kind of association may be necessary in order to prevent competition from forcing down prices below the cost of production ; but they insist that the community should provide some guarantee against the prices being, by aid of monopolies, pushed above the cost of production. In all this they are simply applying the rules of the Cost-principle.

By these and other means—among which it should never be forgotten that competition is the most important—modern society is continually approaching a state of things where prices are regulated in accordance with the principles explained in the beginning of this paragraph and deduced from the very purpose of prices. Speaking very broadly, prices *are* already, in modern society, regulated on these principles. It seems therefore natural for the economist who has to explain the general causes governing prices to make the Cost-principle his starting-point. If he proceeds on the assumption that prices are regulated according to this principle, he will be able to show what are the causes governing the " social value " of the various commodities and of every factor of production. And this is, after all, the first point which most of us expect economic science to explain.

Next we may ask : Why do some factors of production not come up to their social value ? why are some paid considerably above that value ? And finally : How shall we manage to bring prices into conformity with social value? The last question carries us into the field of practical economic policy. In a book which has for title the Nature and Necessity of Interest, we shall have something to say about interest-policy. But our main task will naturally be to examine the causes governing the social value of that service for which interest is paid. In order thoroughly to clear up this difficult question, we must first devote some attention to the causes which govern prices in general, assuming that these prices are regulated in accordance with the Cost-principle.

§ 3. *General causes governing prices.*

In an ideal state of things, prices are, as we saw in the last paragraph, subject to the following conditions :—

(1) uniformity of prices of commodities ;
(2) equality between these prices and the cost of production ;
(3) uniformity of prices of factors of production ;
(4) equality between demand and supply.

Now it is contended that these principles are, generally, sufficient for the complete determination of prices. This can be proved mathematically by showing that the prices may be regarded as the unknown in a complete system of simultaneous equations ; and in this manner the general nature of the relations connecting the different economic factors will probably be best explained. But the ordinary student will certainly prefer another way. To put the matter in its simplest form : Let us suppose a society, regulated by the Cost-principle, to have arrived at a state of equilibrium. We have then, in order to prove that our conditions are sufficient for determining the prices, only to show that no price can be altered without the equilibrium being disturbed and forces counteracting the alteration of the price being brought into play. This is however obvious enough. The Cost-principle requires that the price of a product shall not differ from the aggregate prices of the necessary factors of production. Hence it is enough to consider the prices of the primary productive factors.

If the price of such a factor is increased, the price of every commodity the production of which depends on this factor must, according to the Cost-principle, also increase. But then the demand for such commodities will generally fall off, and therefore also the use of the factor in question. Moreover, it happens that the higher price paid for the productive services stimulates the supply of that service. In the state of equilibrium, the demand had just covered the supply ; now, the demand being smaller and the supply greater, the equilibrium is necessarily disturbed, and there are forces brought into play which tend to reduce the price of the productive service. This reasoning applies—at least theoretically—so long as there is any deviation from the equilibrium price. Hence the counteracting forces will not rest before the old equilibrium is restored.

Similarly, if the price of a factor of production is too low, it will prove impossible to satisfy the indirect demand for the factor of production which arises from the aggregate demand for all commodities in the production of which the factor is used. The scarcity of the factor will inevitably force its price up to the former level.[1]

[1] It may be objected that too low a price of one factor can be balanced by too high a price of another factor, so that the price of the product, and therefore the demand for it, will be unaltered. This is conceivable when both factors only are used together and in invariable proportions to one another. But as soon as such

From these very simple observations, it follows
that every price depends, in the first instance, on the
scarcity of that for which the price is paid in comparison with the demand for it.   This universal
principle will in what follows be referred to as the
Principle of Scarcity.

Land is a factor in the production of corn.   But
this factor is not uniform, the fertility of different
pieces of land being very unequal.   Consequently
there cannot be a uniform price for the use of land.
If two acres of land are used for growing the same
kind of crop, there will be a difference between the
prices paid for the productive services of the two
acres exactly corresponding to the difference in the
harvests yielded, an equal amount of labour having
been bestowed upon them.   Generally, when two
similar factors of production serve the same purpose
but with unequal efficiency, the difference between
the prices fetched by the two factors corresponds to
the difference in the produce, other circumstances
being equal.   Thus in the determination of prices
a new principle is introduced which might be called
the *Differential Principle.*   But this principle does
not, as seems to have been commonly supposed,
cancel the principle of scarcity or make it inap-
plicable.   The higher price of the better land is not
the result of the casual existence of a poorer piece
of land ; on the contrary, the poorer land tends by
competition to lower the price of the richer.   And

obviously exceptional conditions are not satisfied, every variation
of the price of one factor must lead to variations of the price of
some products and therefore disturb the equilibrium.—There are
far more general exceptions from the proposition of the text : for
some commodities and services—such as, *e.g.*, those offered by
railways—the cost of production cannot be exactly determined ; in
such cases prices may be arbitrarily fixed between certain limits.
But, obviously, exceptions of this kind do not essentially affect the
prices of the main classes of productive agents and are of a quite
secondary importance in the general problem of social distribution.

the price that land of any quality fetches essentially depends on the scarcity of land of that quality. The old doctrine is this : If there is poor land of all grades in abundance, cultivation will be extended to a point where the crop does not do more than pay the other factors of production, and the price paid for the use of such land will be nil. The price paid for the use of a better piece of land will then be equal to the difference between the produce of such a piece of land and that of the poorest land brought under cultivation. This is all very true. Only, we should not imagine that we have found in this an independent principle determining prices ; for the margin to which cultivation is extended is not fixed beforehand, but depends wholly on the scarcity of the richer land in comparison with the demand for corn. Thus in all cases we come back ultimately to the principle of scarcity.

The higher reward obtained by a factor of production of higher efficiency according to the differential principle is of course a source of income to the owner of the factor. If the factor is a durable instrument of production, such as land, this income will be periodical and is then called *rent*. But the differential principle is in no way essential to the conception of rent ; the ultimate ground for the payment of a rent being always the scarcity of the service afforded.

Land is the chief, but by no means the single instance, of a factor of production fetching a rent. High class business ability is generally very scarce, and is so essential for the prosperity of large enterprises that a high price is paid for it. In so far as this price is paid periodically it may be called a rent. We pay rent also for the use of produced goods, such as for instance houses, on account of their scarcity ; were they not scarce we should never pay anything for their use.

There is another complication of the principle of scarcity to be taken account of. We have hitherto assumed that the methods of production are invariably fixed, so that the quantity required of every separate factor for the production of a certain quantity of a commodity, may be regarded as given beforehand. This is not so in reality. One factor of production may generally within certain limits be substituted for another ; how much shall be used of each of them depends on their prices. The cheaper a factor is, the further it will, other things being equal, push its way in the process of production. The most important case is the substitution of machinery for labour, with which we shall be occupied in the following chapter. Where labour is dear, it will be good economy to substitute machinery to a large extent ; where again labour is cheap, in many cases it will not pay to introduce the same machinery.

There is a very simple rule for the economy of such a substitution. To take a concrete example : Bituminous coal and anthracite may for many purposes be substituted for one another. Which fuel shall be used is in such cases wholly a question of price. Supposing certain prices to have issued in a state of equilibrium, it will be economically necessary to use bituminous coal for some purposes, anthracite for others. But there will, presumably, be some cases where it does not matter which fuel is used : a certain quantity of bituminous coal does technically the same service as another quantity of anthracite ; these quantities may then be indifferently substituted for one another, provided that they cost the same.

Hence the general rule that the quantities which, in the production process, may be substituted for one another at a *"point of substitution"* must bear the same price. In other words, that factor of production of which a greater quantity must be taken, must be cheaper in proportion. Or : the prices of two factors of production must be in inverse proportion to the quantities which may, indifferently, be substituted for one another at a point of substitution.

This rule does not, as economists sometimes seem to think, afford an independent ground for the determination of prices. It would do so if the points of substitution were fixed beforehand. But they are not. How far a certain kind of service will push its way in different branches of production will always ultimately depend on its scarcity. Therefore the principle of substitution does not, any more than the differential principle, annihilate the fundamental principle of scarcity, but merely modifies its application. The principle of substitution implies, just as does the differential principle, an extra condition that prices must satisfy. But such an extra condition is also necessary in order that prices should be determined ; for the methods of production which we had, originally, assumed as fixed, are in reality variable ; and the new conditions afforded by the principle of substitution only correspond to the greater number of variables thus introduced into the problem.

What has been said will perhaps be enough to make clear the general manner in which prices are determined. But some few remarks should be added in order to facilitate the application of the theory to the discussion of actual problems.

The innumerable causes influencing the price of an article may be divided into those that act on the demand for the article and those that act on the supply of it. We should, however, in using this rule, remember that there are always several causes which affect the price of an article, although they do not appear to have any influence on the demand or supply of that article.   A few consecutive bad harvests, *e.g.*, will raise the price of corn. The general demand of the working classes accordingly will be altered, these classes being compelled to spend a larger part of their income on food.   Their demand for most products of manufacture will decrease, and this again will cause a number of factory labourers to be thrown out of employment or cause their wages to be lowered.   This example shows that there are, generally, connections between all economic forces, and that we cannot limit our discussion to the causes *directly* affecting the demand or the supply.   If we would study the forces governing the price of a special article, however, it is always sufficient to investigate all the causes which may have an influence directly or indirectly on the demand or the supply of that article.   This rule, which considerably simplifies the whole investigation, holds true, of course, even in respect to a factor of production.   And we shall apply it when we now proceed to consider more specially that particular factor of production for which interest is paid.

§ 4. *On Interest considered as a price.*

A "factor of production" has been defined as something which is required in the productive process, but is so scarce that the supply of it would not be sufficient, unless the demand for it were checked by a suitable price being exacted for it. There are of course innumerable factors of production.   But they may be conveniently arranged in certain large groups, of which "labour" is the most conspicuous.   It is not, however, our task in the meantime to give a complete analysis of all the factors of production ; we shall have to confine our attention to an examination of that specific factor for which interest is paid.

All economic goods may be divided into two categories, those which satisfy our wants in being consumed at once, and those which afford a series of useful services before they are worn out. Food is an instance of the former category, houses of the second. This line of subdivision is one of the most fundamental in economic science. The price paid for an article of immediate consumption is of course the same as the price paid for the use of this article. This is not so in the case of an article belonging to the second category. The price paid for the single useful service it affords is one thing ; the price paid for the article itself is quite another thing.

The ultimate purpose of every durable article is to afford useful services. These services may be said to be the commodities actually demanded. The article itself is, from this point of view, merely a necessary instrument for obtaining these commodities. Technically, the process of production ends when the house, the ship, or the machine is built, or the furniture made ; but, economically, the process cannot be said to end before it has reached its ultimate purpose, that is to say, before the concrete service for which a price is paid by the consumer, is ready for disposal. The services are in reality the product ; and everything that is required in order to produce them is, from the economist's point of view, a factor of production. Now of course it is necessary to wait before all the services of which durable goods are capable, can be got out of them. It is logically impossible to exhaust a durable article at once. If we could avail ourselves of all the useful services which a house may yield in the course of future years at the very moment it is built, there would be nothing more required than to build the house. But as we cannot —as such a supposition is altogether against common sense—*waiting* becomes an indispensable factor of production of that most useful service which a house affords. Similarly with all other durable articles, whether their services be demanded by the immediate consumer, as in the case of a house, or by the producer, as in the case of a machine : we shall invariably find waiting to be a necessary condition in order to obtain the services rendered by durable goods.

Supposing a set of workmen have built a house, they may themselves wait for the money that the use of the house will bring in year after year for a long time to come. But they may not be willing to do so ; they may prefer to get the reward of their labour at once ; in this case they may find another person willing to take over the function of waiting in their place. This man will then buy the house ; the workmen will immediately get their wages ; and the buyer will settle down to wait. This shows that waiting is a quite separate function of economic life. It may be taken over by any one who chooses to do it ; but there can be no doubt about the fact that somebody must do it.

So far we have found waiting to be necessary for the consumption of durable goods. It may be added that this purpose is by far the most important source of the demand for waiting. But it is not the only one. There is another reason which makes waiting a necessary element in the economy of society. This reason is that *production*, in the proper technical meaning of the word, *takes time*. Some labour, as *e.g.* that of domestic servants, is of immediate use. But most labour must be performed some time, be it long or short, before the product on which it is bestowed is ready. If labourers were willing to wait till that moment, they would get the price of the product to distribute among them ; they would have, to use a famous term, "the whole produce of their own labour." But generally they do not care to wait, indeed, in most cases, cannot wait ; and they have to find another person to wait in their stead.

It should be observed that we are not, so far, concerned with the question whether anything should be paid for this waiting. The only thing here insisted upon is that waiting is necessary, partly on the ground that the consumption of durable goods takes time, and partly on the ground that production takes time. Between the moment of sacrifice and that of enjoyment a time must elapse ; he who has made the sacrifice must either himself wait for the reward, or he must find some-one else to do it. This necessity is founded on the very nature of things and is not in the slightest degree dependent on social institutions or on any incidental circumstances of our present society. Neither does it seem to have been doubted by any-body ; and the only reason why this point has been dwelt on at some length, is its fundamental import-ance for the whole argument of this book.

In what follows the term "*capital*" will be under-stood to embrace all produced goods except such consumable goods as are already in the hands of the consumer. It might be doubted whether durable goods whose services are of immediate use to the consumer, and which are already in the hands of the consumer, should be termed capital or not. They will in what follows be counted as capital, when the services and the goods themselves, according to prevailing customs in our society, may belong to different persons. Accordingly, houses will be re-garded as capital ; clothing in the hands of the consumer will not. The reason for this distinction is that, in the former case, the consumer has not necessarily himself to take over the function of waiting, while, in the second case, he generally does so. Waiting for the sake of personal consumption of clothing does not influence the market for waiting any more than labour for personal exercise influences the labour-market. It is therefore convenient not to count this sort of waiting. But we have seen, in the first chapter, that waiting is always synonymous with " Use of Capital." This being so, consistency requires that, in cases where the necessary waiting is regularly taken over by the actual consumer, and is therefore not counted as waiting, the corresponding durable goods should not be regarded as capital either.

Produced goods are, as we have seen, of two different kinds : durable goods and consumable goods. According to this subdivision, capital is also subdivided into two categories : *fixed and circulating capital.*

We have found that waiting must be regarded as a separate factor of production. It is also an independent or primary factor in this sense, that it cannot be reduced to more elementary factors. Coal is undoubtedly a factor of production, but not an independent one : it is produced by other factors, principally labour. But waiting cannot in this manner be resolved into more elementary factors ; it is a human exertion of quite a separate and particular character.

That waiting, as a factor of production, must be put on the same footing with all other independent factors, is obvious from the fact that it can be substituted for other factors. We shall have to examine this question at length in the next chapter ; here a single example may be sufficient for illustration. Everybody knows that machine labour may be substituted for hand labour. The service afforded by the machine is not, however, an independent factor of production, but may be resolved into the waiting necessary for obtaining the consecutive services out of the machine and the labour which the production of the machine has required. (We may for the sake of simplicity assume that no other factor has been used in the production of the machine.) Supposing the machine to last for ten years, a tenth part of that labour is consumed every year, and this tenth part is substituted for a certain amount of the former manual labour; but the rest of that manual labour is substituted by waiting.

Further, waiting is a very important factor of production. It is desirable that we should have, in discussing the problem of interest, a general idea of the *rôle* which this factor plays in different branches of production. We have then to remember what was established in the first chapter; that waiting, being synonymous with use of capital, is a quantity of two dimensions, measured by the product of a certain sum of money multiplied by a certain time, the unit for the measurement being the waiting for one pound over one year. Thus a company working with a capital of one million pounds uses yearly a quantity of waiting of one million units. The total yearly expenditure of the company will give a sufficient idea of the importance of all other factors of production taken together. And the comparison between the total capital employed and the total amount of expenditure will show the quantity of waiting used for every pound of expenditure. If such comparisons are made for different branches of industry, they will afford reliable information as to the relative importance of waiting, or use of capital, in these branches.

The following figures are taken from the " Report to the Board of Trade on the relation of wages in certain industries to the cost of production (1891)."

(No more decimals have been quoted than has been thought necessary for the present purpose, and in the third column no decimals have been calculated.)

Description of industry.	Total expenditure. £1,000's	Total capital employed. £100,000's	Use of capital per £ expenditure. £
Firm of Cloth manufacturers ...	25·6	0·017	2/3
Five Coal Companies	650	1·4	2
Gas manufacture, total	11,262	60	5
Tramways in the U.K.	2,267	13·7	6
London and India Docks... ...	1,188	16·1	14
Millwall Dock Co.	131	1·89	14
Southampton Dock Co.	70	1·49	21
Sixteen Railway Companies ...	36,200	718	20
Eight Metrop. Water Companies	661	14·6	22
Canals and Navigations not belonging to Railway Companies.			
Total, United Kingdom	949	24·3	26
Birmingham Canal Navigations...	84	3·6	43
Aire and Calder Navigation ...	46	2·43	53
Regent's Canal, City and Docks Railway Co.	25·7	1·57	61

It will be seen at a glance that waiting is a comparatively small item in industries which work with much circulating capital, but relatively little fixed capital, such as cloth manufacturing;[1] but that waiting becomes a more important factor in branches of production where fixed capital is used to a larger extent. This is in complete accordance with what

[1] According to the German Census of 1895 the following numbers of persons were employed, on an average, by a capital of one million marks (about £50,000):

In the oil and soap industry...	...	...	...	...	38
,, ,, chemical	,,	...	...	...	...	...	57
,, ,, metal	,,	...	...	...	...	...	184
,, ,, machine	,,	...	...	...	...	...	167
,, ,, glass	,,	...	...	...	...	...	196
,, ,, textile	,,	...	...	...	...	...	201

This gives an idea of the relative importance of labour and waiting in different manufacturing branches.

was said above; that by far the greater part of all waiting is required on the ground that the consumption of durable goods takes time, a comparatively small quantity of waiting being required on the ground that production takes time.

If the quantity of waiting required in different branches of production were in nearly the same proportion to the labour wanted, we might imagine that, although a price had to be paid for waiting, this would have no influence on the relative prices of commodities. We should then have a theory of prices in *Ricardian* style, for we could assert that prices of commodities are ultimately regulated by the amount of labour bestowed upon them. But the figures quoted prove that any such assumption is in the most striking contradiction with facts. The proportion of the waiting to the labour embodied in a commodity or a service is liable to the most extreme variations; hence, if a price be paid for waiting, it must have a very material influence on the relative prices of commodities.

We have defined interest as the price of waiting or of the use of capital. It would seem that this price should, like all other prices, be expressed in the unit of money, *e.g.* in pounds. But as the very service which is paid for is itself measured by a certain sum of money used during one year, the price of the service will be determined as a certain fraction of this sum.[1] For this reason the price of waiting or the use of capital is quoted as a "rate," as so much "per cent." This circumstance should, however, not be allowed to obscure the fundamental

---

[1] Waiting is of the dimension Money × Time ($M \times T$). Interest is, as a price, of the dimension Money. Hence the rate of interest is of the dimension $\dfrac{M}{MT} = T^{-1}$. This is the result already arrived at by *Jevons* (Theory of Political Economy, 2nd ed.).

fact that interest is a real price to be placed on the same footing as all other prices.

Having thus traced the general characteristics of the special factor of production called waiting, we now arrive at the central point in the problem of interest. Waiting is a necessary condition of production, or, more generally, of the satisfaction of human wants. There is no doubt about this. But is it also necessary that anything should be paid for waiting? In this question lies the whole problem of interest; for interest *is* the price paid for waiting. The mere fact that waiting is necessary does not prove that interest is also necessary. Sunshine and air are undoubtedly indispensable elements of production; but nothing is paid for them. Why then may not waiting be had for nothing? There are plenty of rich people who do not sacrifice anything by postponing the enjoyment of part of their means, *i.e.* by waiting. On the contrary, it is a great advantage for them to get an opportunity to do so. Why then should they be paid for it?

The answer to these and all the similar questions, which together make up the total problem of interest, is in principle very simple. In the case of a factor of production being scarce when offered gratuitously, a price must necessarily be paid for that factor. The purpose of the price is to check demand and stimulate supply, and therefore the price must be brought up to the level where it causes demand and supply to meet. Consequently, all we have to prove is that waiting would be scarce, if no price, or no sufficient price, were paid for it.

As a matter of fact, at the present time a price is paid for waiting. We shall have to examine the causes governing this price. We have already seen that these causes may be divided into two groups, those affecting the demand for waiting and those affecting the supply of waiting. Accordingly, our

investigations on this question will be divided into
two chapters.   In the next chapter we shall have to
examine more carefully the different sources of the
demand for waiting, and, particularly, to study how
this demand, in its different aspects, is affected by
the principal forces at work in the organic development of economic life.   Similarly, in the succeeding
chapter, we shall have to examine the causes
governing the supply of waiting.   The necessity of
interest being a central point in the argument of
this book, we shall have to devote special attention
to the question : what would happen, if the rate of
interest fell to a very low level ?   We shall find
that both demand and supply would thereby be
affected so seriously that the downward movement
of the rate would necessarily be brought to a stop.
There are, in fact, strong reasons for believing that
the rate of interest will never, for any length of time,
sink below $1\frac{1}{2}$ or even 2 per cent.   If this can be
shown, the necessity of interest may be regarded as
established.

Throughout this whole discussion, we shall assume
that there is only one price for waiting so long as
the conditions of waiting are the same.   In other
words, we shall assume that the perfect market
which is required by the Cost-principle has been
established.   There are in the present world several
forces which compel certain borrowers to pay much
more interest than they would have to pay if an
ideal system of prices prevailed.   We shall not, in
our general discussion of interest, take any account
of such forces ; but limit ourselves to those which
might be supposed to be at work in a society where
the Cost-principle is strictly enforced.   It is easier
to do this in the case of interest than in the case of
any other factor of production ; because the market
for the use of capital is, in spite of everything, the
most perfect of all markets.   By thus limiting the

problem before us we shall not only make the task easier, but we shall also have this advantage, that our results are independent of the deficiencies of the present economic organisation and would in the main be valid even under an ideal system of prices. This is, of course, of great importance if we would strike at the very root of the objections against interest.

There might, however, still be some doubt as to whether, after all, the validity of this deduction does not ultimately depend on the tacit assumption that the present form of society will last. It may be admitted that interest is necessary in the present state of things. But if our old society, with its private ownership of the means of production, be abolished, and a new society on socialistic lines constructed, would it not then be possible to do away with interest in every form, and secure to the labourer " the whole produce of his labour." This is the argument of the Socialists. If it were true, the necessity of interest would be a very relative one and could not claim to have its roots in the very nature of economic things. It is, therefore, thought advisable to meet the Socialists on their own ground ; to assume the socialistic society to be established ; and to prove that even there, interest would be demanded and would have to be paid. If this can be proved, there will be no room left for doubt as to the absolute and unconditional necessity of interest.

CHAPTER III

§ 1. *Waiting for consumption of durable goods. Principle of Scarcity.*

THERE are, as we have seen, two principal sources of demand for waiting, viz. that the consumption of durable goods takes time, and that production takes time. There is, besides, a third source of minor importance, viz. the personal desire of some individuals to consume at present what they will not acquire until later. The examination of these three sources of demand for waiting is the object of the present chapter. We shall begin with the first and most important of them.

Durable goods are of two different kinds ; (1) those whose use immediately satisfies human wants ; (2) those whose use is demanded only as an instrument in the production of other commodities which may, directly or indirectly, satisfy those wants. This distinction is not, however, very essential—at any rate for the problem of interest ; neither is the line of division very sharp. Railways are used for the immediate convenience of passengers as well as for the transport of the materials of industry ; the same applies in the case of streets, roads and ships. Houses may be used, alternatively, as

dwellings or as workshops, or perhaps for both purposes at once.   The use of all durable goods may,
therefore, be conveniently dealt with under one
heading.

Now we have seen that the use of durable goods
requires, in all cases, a certain amount of waiting,
the different uses being necessarily consecutive.
From this necessity arises the larger part of the
demand for waiting.

This demand for waiting depends of course, in
the first instance, on the demand for the immediately
useful services of durable goods and for the commodities produced by means of durable instruments.
If such demand should increase, there would
necessarily be an increase in the demand for waiting.
For instance, if a country like China became aware
of the great advantages to be derived from a
system of railways, there would be a new and
considerable demand for waiting in that country.
Again, some commodities require for their production a much greater amount of durable instruments than others ; the manufacture of gas requires
more than that of cloth, the water-supply in towns
requires still more.   A special increase in the demand
for such commodities, as compared with that for other
commodities, will therefore, other things being equal,
cause an increase in the demand for waiting.

Thus the demand for the use of durable goods
—whether for production or for immediate enjoyment—is always, indirectly, a demand for waiting.
Supposing, then, the supply of waiting to be given,
its price will be determined by the fluctuations of
this indirect demand.   And, *vice versa*, the demand
for the use of durable goods will be regulated by the
price which has to be paid for waiting, this price
acting always as a check on demand—cutting off
demands of less urgent necessity.   How far the
demand can be satisfied, and what price must be

reached in order to restrain the demand within this limit, depends, on the one side, on the intensity of the demand, on the other side, on the scarcity of the supply.

In this statement, which is wholly on the lines of the Principle of Scarcity, lies the fundamental explanation of the phenomenon of interest.

It is to be observed that we have to do here not only with a certain quantity of durable goods demanded, but also with the durability of the goods. If goods of greater durability are demanded, there will, as a rule, be an increase in the demand for waiting, for, in general, greater durability cannot be obtained without extra labour being bestowed on the goods. Suppose a country were to substitute brick houses for wooden houses or for some still more perishable kind of building, and suppose that the new kind of houses cost as much again as the old, then, for the same quantity of house-accommodation, double the amount of waiting would be required.

From what has just been said, it is clear that the future of the rate of interest very much depends on the development of the demand for durable goods. There are strong reasons for believing that this demand will go on increasing as it has done hitherto. The most conspicuous and, in our times, one of the most important reasons for the steady increase of the demand for durable goods is the growth of population. For every new family a new house is required; with the house follows the necessity for furniture, for an extension of the water or gas supply, for streets, perhaps even for new railway or tramway lines. The expenses in connection with house-accommodation for an increase in population are numerous and large, and are almost all of such a nature as to necessitate a great deal of waiting. To these must be added other needs of the additional population, the satisfaction of which generally requires that factories, machinery, tools, etc., should be increased at the same rate as the population itself. As these additions to the existing stock of durable goods usually embody the latest improvements and are therefore produced at a greater cost than the average of the corresponding goods already existing, the demand for waiting will increase even faster than the population. Consequently, so long as population goes on increasing, it is plainly impossible that the demand for waiting, or for the use of capital, should be satisfied by the stock of capital already accumulated. Unless this stock is augmented at least in the same proportion as the population, things will inevitably come to a state of stagnation or even retrogression. In a condition of rapid progress the demand for waiting must necessarily grow much faster than population.

The progress with which we are concerned at present is a progress in the nature of desires and needs. In England and some other highly civilised countries, there is among the upper classes a large demand for good and therefore expensive houses and for furniture of the same character. It seems reasonable enough to assume that such demand will spread even to the lower classes, and to other countries where the great middle class is still content with dwellings of inferior quality. And the spread of such wants cannot but call forth a strong demand for waiting. It is a common complaint that the labouring classes, even in this country, spend so much of their money on articles of immediate enjoyment such as tobacco and alcohol, but cannot be induced to pay much for house accommodation or home comfort. If a change of demand took place in this highly desirable direction among the labouring classes, it would cause an enormous increase in the demand for waiting, and therefore, presumably, also some rise in the rate of interest.

In the same way, the railway systems of this country and of some continental states are fairly well developed ; but in most countries of the world very much remains to be done before we have exhausted the possibility of building railways capable of yielding the rate of interest now prevailing in England. There is already much demand for such means of communication ; and as new countries, *e.g.* South Africa, are opened up and new centres of population created, as civilisation spreads and security of life and property becomes established in old and well-populated countries such as Japan and China, Turkey and Persia, this demand must evidently increase very considerably. Owing to several circumstances, European capitalists are not willing to invest capital in countries of the character here referred to, unless they can count on a much higher rate of interest than that prevailing at home. But as a matter of fact there may be said to exist in the most modern business enterprise a strong tendency to break down the boundaries of countries and nations, and to make the whole world a uniform field for its operations. As this end is gradually brought about, and capital therefore supplied on more equal conditions in the different markets, the demand for durable goods must grow enormously.

The extensive railway building in Europe in the period 1850 to 1870 unquestionably caused a rise in the rate of interest. In our day the same seems to be the case in the numerous applications of the science of electricity, among which the electrical tramways have perhaps absorbed the largest amount of capital. We seem justified in assuming that the same inventions, when applied over the whole world, will have a similar influence on the market for the use of capital. Surely the work which remains to be done simply in order to provide the world sufficiently with the durable instruments of transport will give employment to very much of the fresh capital which will come on the market in the twentieth century.

To give a forecast of the future development of science and of its technical applications, has always proved rather a disappointing task. But experience shows that we are more likely to be on the safe side if we assume such progress to be unlimited. What we know is that new wants are steadily being created by new inventions, and that these inventions generally require the use of a great amount of durable goods. The telephone is a good instance : the present generation has, through this invention, acquired a new want which can be satisfied only by the use of considerable capital. Thus fresh sources of demand for waiting are continually added to those already existing. On this account the demand for waiting will grow as long as there is any such thing as scientific progress.

To sum up the argument, we might say that there are four general tendencies in economic life, increasing the demand for durable goods. The first of these, the growth of population, is nearly wholly out of reach of the influences of a conscious social policy, and must, therefore, from the point of view of the problem of interest, be regarded as a given and necessary tendency. The remaining three, viz. the spread of civilised wants to all classes of population, and to all nations, and the higher development of such wants through the progress of science, are, so far as they may be influenced by any conscious policy, highly desirable items in the programme of Social Evolution. And as to the future of these tendencies, it is fairly certain that they will remain as strong as they are to-day for at least some generations to come ; the last of them indeed, being dependent on scientific progress, probably for ever.

Such, then, are the chief tendencies of economic

life with regard to the use of durable goods. All of them point to a continuous growth of the demand for waiting. This truth is one of the fundamental facts upon which the theory of interest has to be built.

There are, however, certain forces working in the opposite direction ; and although these do not affect the conclusions we have arrived at, they should not be overlooked. There is a natural tendency to economise waiting just because something must be paid for it. In the case of durable goods, this tendency manifests itself in an effort to get the services out of a durable instrument as soon as possible. Now the time within which this may be done is only in certain instances and within narrow limits dependent on human will. It is possible, however, to wear out machinery and other durable instruments of production in a shorter time by using them more continuously. In this way a considerable amount of unnecessary waiting may be saved. The division of labour, as already pointed out by *Rae*, has a certain tendency in this direction,[1] for, so long as the same labourer has to do several different kinds of work, he generally finds it necessary to use many different tools, and most of these must naturally lie idle for the greater part of the time ; whereas, where there is a complete division of labour, the various tools are in continuous use. Thus waiting is saved. But it is clear enough that the diminution in the demand for durable goods which might result from this is confined within very narrow limits, and that, so far as division of labour goes, most industries have already reached the limits. Hence, the division of labour will not, in the future, appreciably check the general tendency towards an increasing demand for durable goods.

[1] New Principles of Political Economy ; Boston 1834. Book II., Ch. VIII.

The question how to save waiting through more continuous use of the durable instruments of production has, however, another aspect which seems to have greater practical importance in our age. A considerable part of our factories, collieries, mines, etc., are not worked more than from eight to ten hours out of the twenty-four. It would surely have an injurious effect on the labourer if the work in all these industries were continued throughout the whole twenty-four hours, say, for instance, on the three-shift system. The same, however, can hardly be said as regards the system of working in two shifts of eight or nine hours each; but such a plan, if generally applied, would involve a very considerable saving in the use of durable goods and therefore of waiting. Suppose all the factories in a country to be worked one hundred hours in the week instead of fifty as before, then, for the same output, not more than half the number of durable instruments, such as factory buildings, machinery, and tools would be required. How far such a system is practicable can of course only be decided by experts in the different branches of production. The only point insisted upon here is that, if this were possible, half of the fixed capital used in the industry of the nation would be saved, and would therefore be free for new enterprises or for a higher technical development of the industries already existing. Such an enormous abundance of capital could not, however, fail to influence the market in favour of labour and to the disadvantage of the owners of capital. Or, in the terms here adopted, the abundant supply of waiting, in comparison with the demand for it, could not fail to reduce the price of waiting, *i.e.* the rate of interest; and, inasmuch as a low rate of interest is to the advantage of the labouring classes, they would necessarily profit thereby. Of course, this truth is liable to several modifications and limitations in actual life; but the leaders of working men should never altogether lose sight of it.

Some durable goods, as for instance bridges, are physically capable of yielding an almost unlimited number of services; but the actual use made of them is often very small, being wholly dependent on the frequency with which they are employed. The principal railway bridges in London are used, at least during some hours of the day, to well-nigh their utmost traffic capacity, but, in the north of Sweden, there are railway bridges which are not used by more than four or six trains in the twenty-four hours. The average use of capital, which attaches to each useful service in these two cases, differs enormously, and is much smaller in the case of an intense traffic of a concentrated population like that of London than it is in districts with a thin and widely spread population. The demand for waiting—as compared with the demand for useful services—must, on this ground, always be relatively smaller in densely populated places. In so far as there is a general tendency for population to increase all over the world, we might expect as the result of this a relative diminution in the demand for waiting, but as, at the same time and for the same reason, human wants are most likely to increase absolutely, we are not justified in assuming that, on this account, the total quantity of waiting demanded will diminish.

There is, of course, waste of waiting just as there is waste of every other factor of production. But this fact does not in any way disprove the truth that interest depends on the scarcity of waiting; neither does it prove that interest could be dispensed with, if there were no waste of waiting. For, firstly, there is in the whole province of economics no such thing as absolute economy; there must always be some waste, just as there must always be some weakness and some mistake in all individual action and some insufficiency in all organisation. In every discussion, therefore, which claims to have any practical bearing whatever, a supposition to the effect that there should be absolute economy in the use of a special factor of production, or in any branch of production, is entirely out of place.

Secondly, we must consider the question : What is waste of waiting ? There is much waste of capital in our present society. The reasons for this are not difficult to find. Under the so-called system of Free Competition there is, and always must be, in certain branches of production, a tendency to create such a quantity of durable instruments as will meet the very maximum of demand. The upward movement of the market having reached its culmination, the durable instruments of production, the ships, factories, machinery, etc., remain. These instruments, therefore, are very often far in advance of the actual demand. On this peculiar side of our economic life, much light has recently been thrown by the various forms of industrial organisation, undertaken in order to avoid the disastrous effects of the tendency just referred to. The *cartels*, trusts, and other "combines" of industrial enterprises have often been able to dispense with a considerable amount of the durable instruments taken over : the case of the American Whisky Trust, abandoning at once sixty-eight out of eighty distilleries, and still fully capable of meeting the demand, is very significant.

Hence it is fairly evident that there is great waste of capital traceable to deficiencies in the economic organisation of our present society. There is also a large amount of waste which depends mainly on other circumstances ; for instance, a great deal of capital is spent on useless and ill-advised experiments. It is, therefore, quite conceivable that we might reach a state of affairs where a much better economy of capital would prevail. It must, however, be remembered that waste of concrete capital is waste of the labour bestowed on that capital, just as much as it is waste of waiting. Less waste of capital means an increase in the "national dividend." For the labour, waiting, and other factors of production, previously used in creating unnecessary capital, will now be used in some more fruitful way, for instance in producing durable instruments for new branches of production. And it is altogether impossible to say, in general terms, how the demand for waiting and the rate of interest would be thereby affected. Thus the possibility of diminishing the waste of capital, though it proves the possibility of a more complete satisfaction of human wants, proves nothing as regards the rate of interest.

Finally, even if a more rational organisation of social production were accompanied by a certain decrease in the demand for the use of durable goods, and consequently, for waiting, this effect could not last very long ; because, once the more rational system were established, the very cause for the decrease of the demand would have disappeared.

Summing up, then, our examination of the tendencies which might have some influence in diminishing the demand for durable goods, we must say that these tendencies are all confined within comparatively narrow limits, and that, when these are reached, their effect on the demand for durable goods disappears. Those tendencies, however, which have been found to increase the demand for durable goods have a much wider range. Hence we may conclude that the demand for waiting, so far as it depends on the demand for the services of durable goods, will, in all probability, continue to increase for at least so long a time as the present generation need at all concern itself with.

So far we have not taken into consideration the possibility of a fall in the price that has to be paid for waiting. If such a fall were to take place, it is clear enough that the demand for durable goods would be greatly stimulated thereby. But any such increase in the demand would necessarily react upon the price and check any further fall. If therefore we wish to refute the general opinion that the rate of interest has a necessary and unlimited tendency to fall and will ultimately equal zero, we shall have to examine the probable effects of a serious fall in the rate of interest, say, for instance, to $1\frac{1}{2}$ per cent., on the demand for waiting, and, particularly in this paragraph, on the demand for durable goods.

Let us take, for instance, houses—the most important of all durable goods of immediate use. The rate of interest has a considerable influence on the yearly rent of houses. It is true that in the case of a house in the City of London, or in the centre of any other great town, the ground-rent is by far the most considerable item in the total annual sum paid for the use of a house. But such cases are exceptional, and in general, the interest on the capital invested in the building is the chief item in the house-rent. Supposing, for instance, the rate of interest to be $4\frac{1}{2}$ per cent. and the total sum of all other yearly expenses to amount to $1\frac{1}{2}$ per cent. of the capital value of the house, then, if the rate of interest were reduced to $1\frac{1}{2}$ per cent., the house-rent would be reduced from 6 to 3 per cent. of the value of the house. This assumption of the reduction of house-rent to one half is perhaps excessive ; but the reduction of the house-rents in any country even to something like one half of the present day figures would undoubtedly call forth an enormous increase in the demand for house accommodation ; for, since this is one of the most intense forms of demand, it has a large capacity for expansion.

At a very low rate of interest not only would more houses be required, but houses of quite another quality. It would cost but a trifling extra sum in annual rent to build a house of the very best materials ; it is even conceivable that such a house would cost less, the expenses of yearly repair and the instalments on the sinking fund being diminished —but this question falls under the Principle of Substitution, which will be considered in the next paragraph. Under such circumstances, however, a general preference would be given to the most durable houses, on the ground that they looked better and were more comfortable to live in ; and this could not but affect the demand for waiting very materially.

A serious fall in the rate of interest would have a similar effect on the demand for all commodities or services for which a large quantity of durable instruments is required. There is in all countries, and especially in the thinly populated ones, an enormous demand for railways which will not pay so long as the rate of interest is 4 or 5 per cent., but which would pay, and therefore would be built, if the rate of interest went down to something between 1 and 2 per cent. In fact, there is practically an unlimited demand for durable goods in general. This is just one of the most essential reasons why the rate of interest remains at its present height : the demand must be restrained within such limits that it can be satisfied by the available supply of waiting. Thus even a slight fall in the rate of interest would create plenty of opportunities for investing capital in durable goods.

These considerations show the absolute absurdity of thinking that the rate of interest could ever go down to zero. The chief cost in using very durable goods is at the present time the interest on the capital invested in them. If this principal item were reduced to zero, or even to a small fraction of what it now is, there would be no luxury whatever in the way of substantial and expensive buildings and furniture, or any other durable goods, which people would deny themselves. The governments of all countries in the world would be enabled to double their naval forces and treble their fortresses. The pipe-systems for gas and water supply could be extended to every cottage in the country districts ; submarine tunnels would prove a very profitable undertaking, not only under the English Channel, but under a great many other waterways in the world. For the financial burden of the original costs on each year's budget would be practically *nil.* The reader might add any number of similar instances, even if he confined himself to present technical possibilities. But we should not forget that the entire technical science of our age has been developed under the condition that something must be paid for the use of capital, and that this factor is, therefore, to be strictly economised ; if this condition could be dispensed with, entirely new lines would be opened up for the development of technical processes.

It would, however, be useless to consider further the extravagances in which social economy would indulge, if nothing were to be paid for the use of capital. Long before the rate of interest reached the zero point, those needs and desires which require the use of durable goods would have been satisfied out of all proportion, while other wants would have been neglected. Far too great a part of the productive capacity of society would in this way have been directed towards the manufacture of goods whose use would lie, essentially, in the future ; and this could not fail to make the satisfaction of present wants rather meagre. This want of proportion between the satisfaction of future and of present wants would, inevitably, affect the very desire of providing for the future, that is to say, the supply of waiting ; and thus the fall in the rate of interest would very soon be brought to a standstill. This is, however, a point which we shall have to consider, more particularly, in the next chapter.

§ 2. *Waiting for consumption of durable goods. Principle of Substitution.*

The rate of interest has a considerable influence on the relative prices of different commodities and services. Hence, as the rate of interest varies, some commodities will replace others in the demand of the consumers ; and this variation of the demand will, again, react upon the rate of interest. This part of our problem we have already discussed in the last paragraph.

The rate of interest has however an important bearing on the question : What technical methods are to be used in order to satisfy a given want? This question is, of course, always determined to a certain extent on purely technical grounds ; but it is also, within wide limits, a question of prices. If two methods are available, that one which is cheaper should be—and is generally—used. And if two factors of production may be substituted for one another, that one is employed whose working is cheapest.

Now, we have seen that the use of durable goods implies waiting. Waiting is for this purpose a factor of production which can be substituted for nearly any other factor or group of factors. When land is

so dear that railway companies prefer underground
lines, a substitution of waiting for the use of land
takes place. It might be argued that it is the labour
required to make the tunnel which is substituted for
the use of land.   We are not concerned, here, however, with the cost of the tunnel, but with the cost
of the use of the tunnel.   This resolves itself on
the one hand into the yearly expenditure for keeping
it in repair, and for laying aside an annual instalment
in order to make up for its depreciation of value,
and, on the other, into the price that has to be paid
for waiting.   The first two items together would
probably not exceed the corresponding costs on
the open line ; so that in this case waiting and
nothing else is substituted for the use of land.

Again, let us suppose that the price of land is of
no importance, and that the tunnel is built in order to
avoid the greater traffic expenses on an alternative
open line, and, further, that the annual sum to be set
aside for depreciation is the same for both lines ;
then there is a clear substitution of waiting for the
whole group of factors of production paid under the
heading " surplus traffic expenses on the open line."
These expenses being given, the question whether
such a substitution ought to take place or not depends
wholly on the price of waiting, that is to say, on the
rate of interest.   This point however seems sometimes to be very much neglected by those who have
to lay out new railway lines.

A local board might be in doubt whether to build
a bridge cheaply, to last for fifteen years only, or
at double the expense, to last for sixty years.   We
might, for the sake of simplicity, assume the cost
of repairs to be the same in either case.   Then it
is clear that, in the case of the more expensive
bridge, a larger sum has to be paid on account of
waiting, and a less on account of depreciation.
Hence a certain quantity of waiting might be said

to be substituted for other factors included in
" bridge-building." The kind of bridge to be built
will, again, depend wholly on the rate of interest.
The calculation is simplest if we suppose the board
in either case to cover the cost by a loan repayable
by an annuity for a fixed period ; we have then
only to examine which of the annuities at a given
rate of interest is larger, that for a loan of one
pound to be paid back in fifteen years, or that for a
loan of two pounds to be paid back in sixty years.
The calculation shows that the annuities are nearly
equal when the rate of interest is $4\frac{1}{8}$ per cent. With
a higher rate it will prove more advantageous to
build the bridge on the cheaper plan ; but if the rate
be lower than $4\frac{1}{8}$ per cent. the more expensive bridge
will be preferred.

These examples are perhaps sufficient to give
a clear conception of the nature and economy of
substitution. We have now to examine the general
tendencies of economic life with regard to the substitution of the use of durable instruments, and
therefore of waiting, for other factors of production.

1. It may be said at once that there is, on the
whole, a strong tendency in this direction. In the
first place the *development of technical science* gives,
almost daily, a wider field for the use of durable
instruments. It is only natural that such should be
the case. For almost all the efforts of inventors
are directed towards finding durable instruments
to do the work which has hitherto been done by
hand. The original expenditure to be incurred may
be great, but as this outlay is spread over a large
number of uses, the cost of each use is very small
as compared with the cost of hand labour. If advantage could be taken to its full extent of this
principle, there would be, practically, no limit at all
to this kind of substitution. But, as waiting has
to be paid for, there is at any one time a limit

to the application of the principle referred to ; this
limit being essentially regulated by the rate of
interest.

Not all inventions have for purpose the replacing
of hand labour by machinery, or, more generally,
the replacing of successive acts of labour by a greater
labour expended once for all. Methods of production may be improved as well by substituting
new and more efficient machinery for that which is
out of date. The new machinery being presumably
more expensive, its introduction will, other things
being equal, involve a greater demand for waiting.

Although the tendencies of technical progress lie
chiefly in this direction, we must not overlook the
fact that there is a third kind of progress which has
quite an opposite effect, namely, that of diminishing
the quantity of durable goods required for production.

This arises from the possibility of attaining the
same end by means of durable goods of a less
expensive nature ; the substitution of the Marconi
system of telegraphy for that by cable being perhaps
the most striking instance. But it is obvious that
the scope for such progress is not, and indeed cannot
be, very extensive, whereas that for the use of *more*
expensive instruments is limited only by the price
to be paid for the waiting required.

2. Proceeding now in our analysis of the tendencies of economic life, as regards the substitution of
durable instruments for other factors of production,
we find secondly a large and characteristic movement
in favour of such substitution, viz. the *concentration
of industry*. This movement includes, on the one
side, all kinds of combines, from the German
"Cartel," with its relative independence of the
combining parties, to the American "Trust," which
practically forms a single business ; and, on the
other side, the Cooperative Movement. All these
tendencies, different as they are in other respects,

have essentially the same bearing on the development of the technical methods of production.

The Danish peasant has, solely through his splendid system of cooperation, secured the assistance of the most modern and efficient dairy machinery, which would have been of no advantage to him if isolated. Cooperation in this case may be said to have directly created a fresh demand for the use of durable instruments.

Similarly in the case of the Standard Oil Company. So long as the oil industry was divided among many small firms, oil was carried in wooden barrels. With the greater concentration of the industry special railway trucks were built for transporting the oil in tanks ; but only in virtue of a gigantic combination of the interests involved would it have been possible and profitable to construct that extensive system of pipe lines by which the Standard Oil Company now transports its oil. The same applies to the European import of paraffin oil. As of late this business has, in most countries, been monopolised by some few firms, it has become possible to construct special tank steamers from which on arrival the oil is pumped directly into large tanks. This method of transport involves the investment of a considerable amount of capital in durable instruments. But it is undoubtedly cheaper, as variations of wages and of the rate of interest within reasonable limits do not in the least affect the superiority of the method. There was, consequently, only one condition necessary to make the method practicable ; this condition was the concentration of the import business in a few hands. A small importer could never use a tank steamer ; he was not likely to order enough at a time to freight such a steamer ; and, even if he were able to do so once in the year, he would probably wish to get the oil in the autumn, when no such steamer is to be had ; or he would have to charter the steamer for the whole year in order to use it once. Hence the inferiority of the small importer may be said to consist in his incapacity for using up all the services which the durable instrument affords.

This statement at once makes it clear why industrial concentration must stimulate to such an extent the substitution of the use of durable goods for other factors of production.[1]

The frequency with which durable instruments can be used has arithmetically the same importance for the question of substitution as the rate of interest : a rise of the rate of interest is counterbalanced by a proportional increase of the frequency of use. Practically the variations of the rate of interest are often even of *less* importance. This is specially conspicuous in agriculture. In Germany a horse raker is calculated to pay if it can be used in 2·3 days a year, the rate of interest and of wages being supposed to be 4 per cent. and two marks (about two shillings) a day.[2] Under such circumstances the very small farms cannot use horse rakers. Any variations of the rate of interest which are at all likely to occur will not considerably extend such use, whereas the continual progress of

---

[1] Of course industrial concentration in many cases means better economy in the use of durable instruments. In glove-cutting, a machine is used which does part of the work, the remainder being done by hand labour. One machine can keep 200 labourers at work, but it pays a small employer to use a machine, even if he does not employ more than one or two cutters. This is sometimes done, though it involves of course a great waste of waiting. Thus glove-making affords an instance of an industry where greater concentration would mean a *fall* of the demand for the use of durable goods. It is, however, obvious that such cases can have no great influence on the total demand for waiting. Comp. above, p. 106.

[2] Comp. *G. Fischer:* Die sociale Bedeutung der Maschinen in der Landwirtschaft ; Schmoller's Forschungen Bd. XX, Heft 5. 1902.

co-operation makes the advantages of agricultural machinery accessible for even the smallest farmer.

3. There is a third tendency of modern economic life pointing to an extension of the use for durable instruments of production. This is the *organisation of credit*. There may be ever so much machinery, the economy of which has been established beyond all doubt, and yet it may be beyond the reach of producers who, through lack of credit, are unable to provide the capital required. Such producers might, nevertheless, be worthy of credit. In fact, the movement for the "organisation of credit," which is so remarkable a feature of our time, tends to provide everybody with the credit he is worth. Hence it is obvious that this movement, in its later development, will have a considerable influence on the demand for waiting. This is specially the case with regard to agriculture. Small farmers might not only be enabled to use the best agricultural implements, but also to invest much capital in the improvement of their land and in taking new land into cultivation—were they only able to borrow the necessary money. We have here, indeed, an enormous field for the profitable use of capital, and the only condition necessary for making this latent demand for waiting effective is the organisation of credit.

4. Finally, we have to note a fourth and most important tendency of economic life, pointing to a continuous extension of the use of durable instruments of production, viz. the *rise of wages*. If the same end can be attained just as well by immediate labour as by the use of durable instruments, the price of labour compared with that of waiting will decide which method shall be used. Supposing the rate of interest to be constant, the more expensive labour becomes, the greater will be the substitution of waiting for it.

There are several facts which indicate that such a substitution takes place on a large scale. We shall invariably find that those countries where wages are highest stand first as regards invention and application of machinery. Europe has become accustomed, during the last decades, to look to America for all kinds of automatic labour-saving machinery. No one can doubt that the higher level of wages on the other side of the Atlantic has been a most important cause of American superiority in this field. It is also highly instructive to compare the methods of agriculture in different parts of the world. In India and Russia, where wages are extremely low, agriculture is generally carried on by means of implements of the very simplest description : Australia and the United States are the countries of the steam-plough.

It is reasonable, therefore, to suppose that the rise of wages which may be expected to take place in the old countries will very considerably widen the field for the use of machinery, and that this tendency, so far as it goes, will add its effect to those of the other three we have already considered.

In theory the use of machinery may be resolved into "labour" and "waiting," so that the introduction of machinery may simply be described as a substitution of a certain portion of waiting for labour. But in reality this is not so. When we ask whether a new machine will pay or not, the price of the machine, and generally also several expenses connected with the use of the machine, e.g., those for oil or coal, must be regarded as given beforehand. If this is the case, the only prices which have any influence on the question are the wages for *that special labour* which is replaced by the machine, and the rate of interest which the employer of the machine has to pay. Prices of agricultural machines do not differ considerably from country to country ; but wages of agricultural labourers are extremely different. Therefore the extension given to the use of machinery in agriculture depends mainly, not on the price of " labour " in general, but on the wages prevailing in agriculture.

Most machines are soon worn out, so that the annual depreciation is very considerable. The costs of running the machine are another important item. In comparison with these items interest is, as a rule, an item of secondary importance. Again, in the case of hand labour, the cost of production almost exclusively depends on the rate of wages. We shall therefore generally find that a rise of wages in a special occupation has a much greater influence on the profitableness of the use of machinery than a corresponding fall of the rate of interest.

For instance, if a raker [1] can be used for 2·3 days, the daily expenses are 9 60 marks, the rate of interest and of wages being supposed to be 4 per cent. and two marks a day. If hand labour is used the costs are the same. A rise of the rate of interest from 4 to 5 per cent. adds only 0·52 marks to the daily expenses under the machine method. But if wages rise 25 per cent. (from 2 marks to 2·50 marks), the cost of the hand method is increased by 2·40 marks and that of the machine method by 0·50 marks, so that the difference in favour of the machine method is 1·90 marks. The machine method will therefore easily bear a rise of the rate of interest, if only wages increase in a similar proportion.

In the case of a reaper, the machine method costs as much as the old hand method if the machine can be used two and a half days a year.[2] The price for a day's work is then 41 80 marks, to which are added only 2·20 marks for a rise of the rate of

[1] Comp. above, p. 115.
[2] Comp. *Fischer*, loc. cit. p. 16.

interest of 1 per cent. But if wages rise 25 per cent., 10·45 marks are added to the cost of the hand method and about 3·75 marks to that of the machine method, so that the difference in favour of the latter is 6·70 marks. In comparison with this sum, the extra expenses caused by a similar rise of the rate of interest are insignificant.

In this examination of the tendencies of economic life with regard to the use of durable instruments, a group of circumstances of a more irregular character should also be mentioned.

Even where it is certain that an investment of capital in durable goods will pay, and where the capital may be had without any difficulty, we very often find the use of durable goods much less than it economically ought to be. There are no real reasons here why the substitution does not take place except dulness, lack of activity and of business-like management, and all those thousand obstacles which the theoretical economist usually summarises as "friction." This friction is, however, very considerable. In some old established and highly developed staple industries, such as the cotton manufacture of Lancashire, new machinery seems to be adopted as soon as it has been found to pay. But this is very far from being the case in all branches of industry.

The linotype machine saves much hand labour in newspaper printing offices, and the substitution of machinery for labour is in this case undoubtedly very profitable. In a Gothenburg newspaper office it was stated on inquiry that a clear annual profit of at least $14\frac{1}{2}$ per cent. was made on the three linotypes employed there, and that a much larger profit would have been made, had the machines been more continuously used. In order to fully pay off the machines in twenty years at 5 per cent. interest, an

annual profit of 8 per cent. would have been sufficient.   The weekly wages were about forty shillings
(for forty-eight hours) ; but even if they had not
exceeded thirty shillings, a profit of 10 per cent.
would have been made by the introduction of
machinery ; hence all variations of the wages within
reasonable limits were entirely irrelevant as regards
the profitableness of the substitution.   Despite all
these facts, linotype machines are not yet generally
used in printing offices, or at any rate not to the extent
prescribed by the economic laws of substitution.

At the eastern gas-works of the Corporation of
Copenhagen, a new and thoroughly modern system
of unloading coal has recently been introduced.
For this purpose a capital of about Kr. 500,000 was
required ($£1 = $ Kr. 18).   Under the old method,
when barges were used, the cost of unloading was
Kr. 2·10 per ton.   The use of machinery has
reduced this sum to Kr. 0·47 per ton, including an
annuity of 8 per cent. on the capital invested.   Thus
the sum of Kr. 1·63 is saved on every ton, and, as
the annual consumption of coal amounts to 80,000
tons, there is a clear profit of not less than
Kr. 130,000 over and above the said annuity of
8 per cent.   As the machinery is sufficient for an
import of 100,000 tons a year, the profit will in
time be still greater.   The superiority of machinery
is, in this case, so enormous, that no variations of
wages or of the rate of interest which are at all
likely to occur, can throw doubt on the advantage
of the substitution.   And, although the profits may
vary according to different local conditions, it is
extremely probable that the machine method will
prove superior at every port of any importance.
Nevertheless, there are still, and probably will be
for some time to come, a great many ports where
the unloading of coal is carried on in the old way
by means of barges and hand labour.

Everyone who has had an opportunity of inquiring into the conditions of modern industry must have found how much "friction" retards and limits the introduction of machinery. Perhaps it may be regarded as a tendency of economic life to steadily reduce this element. If this is so, we shall have to take into account a new force, acting in the direction of increasing the demand for durable goods and therefore for waiting.

Summing up our argument, we may say that very important economic tendencies favour the substitution of durable instruments for immediate labour, and therefore increase the demand for waiting. Hence, even a large and continual growth of capital in the future will not necessarily cause a fall of the rate of interest.

Moreover, every fall of this rate will widen the field for the use of durable instruments and thus call out forces counteracting the fall. It is true that, in the case of machinery, interest very often is an item of secondary importance. But as soon as we have to do with instruments of greater durability, such as factory buildings, ships, railways, waterworks, etc., interest becomes a very important item, and, as the larger part of the capital used as durable instruments is of this character, the rate of interest has a very material influence on the methods of production. A substantial fall in the rate of interest could not but convert a great many technical possibilities into economic advantages, and, sooner or later, into realities; and there are absolutely no ascertainable limits to the use of waiting in different branches of production, if that waiting were to be had for nothing.

Waterworks for different purposes seem particularly capable of absorbing vast amounts of capital,[1] and, as they are in general extremely durable, the price paid for waiting is the all-important item in the cost connected with the use of such works. If, therefore, the rate of interest were nil or nearly nil, such enterprises as the Panama Canal would present no financial difficulties. As they would be carried out in such a way as to secure a practically eternal durability, their original cost would be very high ; still, as their use would cost next to nothing, there would be a great demand for them, and they would absorb a considerable part of the fresh capital of the world. In Prussia a scheme for a magnificent system of canals has been drawn up by the government but rejected by parliament. In almost all countries, plans for canals are being discussed which would admit sea-going vessels to the interior. There can be no doubt that such waterways would be constructed on a large scale, and in a most efficient and expensive manner, if the rate of interest were low enough ; moreover, there would be a tendency to diminish steadily the current expenses of such works by spending more money on the original construction. There are, besides, many other kinds of waterworks, which would prove profitable enough at a very low rate of interest, and would absorb enormous amounts of capital. Good instances of such are river-works for the prevention of inundation or for the fertilisation of rainless districts, and the different methods of reclaiming land from the sea or from lakes.

One may say that there is always—lying in stock as it were—any amount of technical possibilities in the way of substituting the use of capital for other

[1] The total sum spent on the waterway of the Elbe, as well as on docks, quays, and other harbour works, since 1888, is reported to have been fifteen million sterling. Much information on the subject is to be found in the Report of the Royal Commission on the Port of London (1902).

factors of production. Every fall in the rate of interest will result in the setting free of a part of these possibilities and the conversion of them into actualities ; and thereby a further fall will be prevented. If in this process the stock occasionally shrinks, it is abundantly compensated for by the continual addition of new possibilities, consequent upon technical progress.

Everyone who attempts to realise the state of things which would accompany a rate of interest of say $1\frac{1}{2}$ per cent. will surely perceive to what an extent the substitution of capital, in the form of durable instruments, for other factors of production, would exceed all we are at present able to supply. The demand for the use of capital for this purpose, which would arise if no interest at all were to be paid for it, must be regarded as practically unlimited ; and the possibility of satisfying such a demand at any future period should not be taken into serious consideration.

§ 3. *Waiting for Production.*

Some time must necessarily elapse between seedtime and harvest. This obvious truth has more than a literal meaning, and is indeed the expression for a very general economic necessity of great importance in the theory of interest. Some difficulties might arise from the question how the time required for any kind of production should be measured, or how to give an exact definition of the " period of production." Happily, we need not trouble ourselves with subtleties like this. Between any single service rendered in a production process and the end of that process, a certain time will elapse ; for this a certain amount of waiting is necessary, and the measure of this is the product of the price of the service multiplied by the time which has elapsed. The sum of all such waiting necessary to a production process is a clear conception and the only one which has any bearing on the problem of interest.

To avoid all ambiguity, however, some things should be added. The term "production" is here taken to include not only production in a purely technical sense but also transport and distribution. Accordingly, "waiting for production" is understood to include, *e.g.*, that kind of waiting which the shopkeeper finds necessary in order to get rid of his goods. Further, when a locomotive is made and delivered to the railway company, this production process is regarded as ended, despite the fact that the use of the engine may become a factor in many future processes of production. Thus it becomes possible to separate waiting for the production from waiting for the consumption of durable goods, and to obtain a clear idea of the total amount of waiting necessary for the former purpose in any production process. This sum of waiting might shortly be termed the waiting required in that production process. Such a sum of waiting may always be regarded as the product of the total amount of money spent multiplied by a certain period of time, and this time may, for the sake of convenience, be called the "period of production" of the process in question. This expression involves a comparison between the actual process and a fictitious one, in which the same total of money is spent but spent at once, the time which elapses between that moment and the moment when the product is ready for use being equal to the period of production. This comparison is obviously justified by the fact that both processes, the real and the fictitious, require the same amount of waiting.

The price paid for the total amount of waiting required in any production process will, of course, enter into the cost of the product, and in this way the price of waiting always has an influence on the demand for different products.[1] This demand again involves a demand for the waiting required in the various production processes and reacts therefore in turn on the price of waiting.

Let us suppose that the same result may be obtained by two processes, differing in their period of production, the shorter process being cheaper when the price of waiting is high and dearer when it is low. It might here be theoretically argued that the rate of interest decides which of these processes shall be adopted, and that a low rate will generally induce people to substitute longer periods of production for shorter ones. It seems, however, extremely doubtful whether the rate of interest has in reality any such influence; in most cases the technical process adopted is absolutely determined by other reasons.

We have now to examine the general tendencies of economic life in relation to the demand for waiting for production. We may state at once that there seems to be a general tendency in the direction of *shortening the periods of production*. This tendency is perhaps most prominent in the process of distribution. Modern methods of communication—such facilities, *e.g.*, as post, telegraph and telephone—tend to accelerate business operations, while the steady increase in speed of transport shortens the time of actual distribution. There is, besides, in the retail trade a growing tendency to diminish the period of turnover, as consequence of the concentration of this trade in very large shops. But production, even in a more technical sense, is continually being shortened through the extended use

---

[1] The prices of old wines, for instance, would be very much reduced by a fall in the rate of interest, and the demand for them would, therefore, in all probability considerably increase.

of modern means of communication and through the concentration of industry into large factories.

There is, in the best organised industries, very little in the way of materials lying idle between two different acts of production, even if these acts have to be carried out in different factories, perhaps at great distances from each other. A modern iron work has no large stock either of raw materials or of their product ; yet there is a continuous stream of ore and coal entering, and of iron being turned out of it. In Prussia, it was recently stated, on an occasion when railway trucks could not be supplied in sufficient quantity, that a great iron work had not more than two days' stock of coal. This shows that the time which elapses from the moment when the coal is found in the earth to that when it is consumed in the production of iron has been shortened to the utmost, the increased reliance now placed upon all kinds of transport arrangements having probably contributed much to these and similar results.[1] A great number of technical improvements have been introduced for the very purpose of shortening the period of production [2] ; and, in nearly

[1] The following figures as to the time required for the production of steel-rails in the Rumlang iron works in Luxembourg are given by an expert :—

	Hours.
From moment of blasting to dump in furnace . .	$\frac{1}{4}$
„ dump to flow of liquid iron	24
„ flow to blast in Bessemer pear (steel). . .	$\frac{1}{2}$
„ blast to rail mill via ovens where temperature of ingots is equalised	2
rolling rails and loading them	$\frac{1}{10}$

Thus about 27 hours are needed to transform iron and coal (from the rough state of nature in which they are found) to steel rails (without holes) loaded on board ship.

[2] A modern shipyard can build a cargo steamer of about 5,000 tons from existing designs and patterns in seven or eight months ; this is, however, very quick delivery, twelve months being a good average time. It is doubtful whether the infinitely smaller and less efficient wooden ships of some generations ago could have been built as quickly.

all progressive methods, such shortening is more or less incidental.   For instance, the steadily increasing speed of machinery cannot but accelerate the whole process of production and thereby diminish the quantity of waiting necessary.   Again, there are, even in agriculture, some interesting instances of shortening.   In Germany, the average age of cattle slaughtered is stated to have fallen steadily during the nineteenth century ; in the case of sheep, for instance, the decrease is reported to be from eight to ten years in the beginning of the century to two to three years at the end.[1]   This tendency, which probably prevails in other countries as well, implies a very considerable reduction in the period of production of meat.   The steadily increasing supply of wheat from the southern hemisphere tends, so far as it goes, to diminish the period of production of bread, reckoning from the moment of harvest, to about one-half.

It should be observed, finally, that business men are becoming more and more accurate in their calculations, and, therefore, more anxious to adopt all schemes for shortening the process of production, provided the interest so saved covers the extra costs incurred.[2]   An illustration of this is afforded by the well-known fact that houses are now built in a much shorter period of time than was usual only a generation ago, and that, in the most advanced instances, all mechanical appliances are used to accelerate the work, electric light even being supplied to admit of night-work.

In conclusion, we may say that economic development tends to reduce the time spent in production and thereby the total amount of waiting required

---

[1] Cf. *Huckert* in Zeitschrift für Socialwissenschaft, 1900.

[2] The modern competition in short delivery has done much, for reducing the period of production, probably even more than the desire to save interest.

for it. It is, however, evident that this tendency cannot go much further. Indeed, it seems probable that the period of production has already in several branches been brought very close to its minimum. We may, therefore, assume that it will never in this way be possible to save any large part of the waiting for production.

So far, we have considered only the element of time. But the element of quantity has just as much effect on the amount of waiting required in production. Now, since this quantity is a steadily increasing amount, and since there are no ascertainable limits to its growth, it follows that there cannot be, at any time, a serious fall in the demand for waiting for production, and that, in the long run, the tendency towards a growth of this demand must outweigh the opposite tendency.

Nor is the whole sum of waiting required from the fact that production takes time very considerable. This kind of waiting corresponds to the use of circulating capital; and the circulating capital is surely only a small part of the whole. Thus, even if a small and temporary fall in the demand for waiting for production took place, in consequence of an acceleration in production, this fall would weigh little in the balance against the continual growth of the use of durable goods.

Summing up then the arguments of this chapter, we arrive at the final conclusion that *the total quantity of waiting required in order to satisfy human wants has a decided tendency to increase; and that a very low rate of interest would stimulate this increase beyond all limits.*

§ 4. *Waiting in Anticipation of Future Incomes.*

Hitherto we have been considering that demand for waiting which arises from the fact of waiting being, objectively and materially, a necessary condition for the satisfaction of human wants. Something still remains to be said about another source of the demand for waiting, and an entirely different one. A person borrowing money at a certain time for consumption in his own household, and repaying it at a later date, undoubtedly makes use of waiting, and adds to the total demand for this service. This waiting is not necessary from the point of view of production. The commodity or service to be consumed is at the disposal of the consuming society. The particular individual, however, who wishes to consume it, has not, for the moment, the means of doing so, but hopes to obtain them at a later period. He, therefore, induces some other person to lend him the money; that is to say, to postpone the enjoyment of that money to the later period; in other words, to take over the function of waiting for him.

The reasons why the borrower should wish for such an arrangement may be quite legitimate. A young man with good natural gifts but without money may wish to enter some profession, for instance that of a medical man; he may, then, with great advantage both as regards himself and society, borrow the money required for his education. If he succeeds, he will be able to pay his debt out of his earnings; and the principal risk, that of the premature death of the borrower, may be covered by an insurance on his life.[1]

There is also, as everybody knows, a large class of debts incurred for personal consumption of quite an illegitimate character. The borrower in such cases consumes to-day a part of some problematical future income which he has no reasonable hope of ever acquiring, and by means of which his future

[1] Such an arrangement is common in Sweden.

wants will be no better provided for than his present ones now are.

To this last category of borrowers belong a good many governments. Indeed, whenever a State increases its debt over and above the total State property, it is clearly guilty of spending anticipated future income. A considerable demand for waiting seems to arise out of such illegitimate anticipations of future resources, and the rate of interest would probably be somewhat lower could we rid ourselves of that particular source of demand.

It seems unnecessary to give further instances of loans for consumption, but some few words should be added as to the general character of such loans. Waiting on the side of the lender enables the borrower to anticipate a future income, *i.e.* to use a future income in order to satisfy a present want. The reverse of this is obviously the postponement of a present income, *i.e.* the use of a present income in order to satisfy a future want; and this is just what we have called waiting. Hence anticipation and postponement are nearly connected with one another, the first being, in fact, only the negative aspect of the second. The reasons for anticipation are therefore as a rule simply the opposite of the reasons for postponement, both being exposed to influences of very much the same character. Since these two lines of action might be regarded as special ways of disposing of individual income, they are, perhaps, from this point of view best studied together.

It is, therefore, not necessary to consider, in this chapter, that demand for waiting which arises from personal expenses in anticipation of future income. This kind of demand may be treated as a negative supply, and may therefore simply be deducted from the supply. As we shall have to examine more carefully, in the next chapter, into the causes governing the supply of waiting, it would only lead to fatiguing repetitions, were we, at this point, to discuss separately the demand for waiting here referred to.

Accordingly we shall in future, when speaking of the demand for waiting, always mean such demand alone as arises from the fact that time is required both for consumption of durable goods and for production.

CHAPTER IV

SUPPLY OF WAITING

§ 1. *On Waiting.*

A MAN who spends only £400 out of an annual
income of £500 is commonly said to *save* £100 per
annum. This sum he might simply lay aside for
future purposes, and thus in time store up a considerable amount in cash. This was indeed the old
method even amongst European nations, and is still
the prevalent custom in some less civilised lands.
In modern society, however, the person who saves
money generally *invests* it.[1] This he may do in
different ways. He may himself make use of it in
his own business, or he may lend it to another person
who is starting business on his own account without
possessing the requisite capital. For the sake of
accurate analysis we shall choose the latter case for
consideration, the function of the person who saves
being there clearly distinguished from that of the

---

[1] This is a necessity in the modern community. As *Sir Robert
Giffen* says : " Saving and investment go on *pari passu.*" If not,
if " the saving community in all directions endeavoured to heap
up its savings in hard cash even for a month, certainly if it did so
for a year, the money market would collapse. The accumulations
of a single year, even taking them at 150 millions only, . . . would
absorb more than the entire metallic currency of the country.
They cannot, therefore, be made in cash."—" Growth of Capital,"
London, 1889, p. 152.

trader ; whereas in the former case both functions, as performed by one and the same person, are confused.[1]

We have studied in the preceding chapter the different purposes for which the employer requires waiting. This waiting is supplied to him by the person who invests money, as investing represents his decision to take over a certain kind of waiting. The employers are the leaders of social industry : it is they who in the first instance decide in what directions the productive forces of the community are to be turned ; though they are, of course, very much limited in their decisions by the wishes of the consumers on the one hand and, on the other, by the willingness of the investors to supply the necessary waiting. If the directors of industry choose to create more capital, *i.e.* if they decide that more durable goods shall be used, or that the volume of production shall be increased so as to necessitate a larger quantity of raw material and intermediate goods, and if the necessary waiting is supplied, then the new capital is created.

Capital is, by definition, *produced*. Hence *accumulation of capital* necessarily involves production of capital. For this production the service of many different factors is required : of these, labour in general is the most prominent. Hence it might be said, with some degree of truth, that "labour has created all capital." But the very existence of that capital when once produced, involves waiting for the sake of the useful services that may be derived from

---

[1] It is clear that the man who undertakes business on his own account, if he is at the same time a capitalist, fulfils in this capacity the same function of waiting as other capitalists. As soon as he is free to decide upon the use of his capital, he might go on contributing his part to the total supply of waiting or he might withdraw it. In this action he will on the whole be guided by very much the same motives as all other capitalists are. Thus his supply is included in the discussion of the present chapter.

it for the satisfaction of human wants, and the decision to supply this waiting must, of course, precede the creation of capital. Saving therefore is a necessary condition for the creation of capital.

The person who saves undoubtedly *abstains* from the consumption of certain commodities or services. From this fact a most curious conception of capital has arisen and caused much confusion in the science of political economy. Capital is regarded simply as an aggregate of these non-consumed commodities, as "a stock of goods of different kinds stored up somewhere," as *Adam Smith* puts it ; and accordingly, it is said, the function of capital is to serve as a fund stored up for the purpose of maintaining the labourers until the fruits of their labour ripen. This view of the matter is entirely erroneous. As a matter of fact, the commodities or services "abstained from" are never produced ; on the whole and broadly speaking, only that is produced which is required by the consumers. If the consumers decide to save and to invest their money in productive enterprises, it means that the industry of the society is diverted to some extent from the production of immediately useful things to the production of capital. Hence saving means diverting productive forces towards future ends.

In many cases a person investing his money must take into account the possibility of losing it. That is to say, there is often a certain element of risk connected with waiting. This element must, in our analysis, be separated, so far as possible, from waiting in the pure and real sense of the term. To incur risk in industrial life is a function by itself, which must be clearly distinguished from the function of waiting. In this chapter we shall have to examine the willingness of people to wait, not their willingness to run risks ; we shall consider therefore only those loans in which there is, practically, no

risk, or, if there is a risk, we shall assume it to be
paid for separately.   There is, of course, in human
life no such thing as absolute security.   Nevertheless, in many transactions of modern society, the risk
is reduced to such a minimum that it is practically
not taken into account.   In these cases nothing is
paid for the risk and therefore all the interest actually
paid may be regarded as reward for waiting.

But, though there may be no difference as to
security, there may be very important differences in
the other conditions of waiting.   Waiting is not a
uniform service, as it is so often represented to be ;
neither is there any such thing as a uniform rate of
interest.

When a person undertakes to supply the waiting
required for a production process, the natural
period for that waiting is at least as long as the
period of production itself ; and, in waiting for the
consumption of durable goods, money would naturally
have to be invested for the whole period of consumption.   Hence it may be said that waiting for
long periods is the real and principal form of waiting.
Waiting for *short periods* is, in relation to this, a
secondary form.   The service performed by this
kind of waiting corresponds only to small parts of a
production process, and most generally to a special
phase of distribution ; and it is only by artificial
means, particularly by the elaborate and ingenious
mechanism of bills of exchange that this form of
waiting has been made possible.

Any contract of waiting may, of course, be taken
over by a third party ; the original lender is therefore bound only until he can find another person
willing to take over his obligations.   But it by no
means lies in the nature of the function of waiting
that such an opportunity should offer itself at every
moment.   By means of a special mechanism, however, this advantage has been secured for a great

class of loans, namely those introduced on the Stock Exchange. It is true that the lender is not guaranteed the return of the precise sum he has lent, the quotations of the Stock Exchange being liable to variations. But even this disadvantage is removed if the money is deposited " on call " with a banker.

It is only natural that waiting offered under such widely differing conditions should command very different prices. In fact, a special rate of interest is quoted for every special form of waiting, the lowest prices generally being paid for waiting "on call " and for waiting under the conditions offered by consols and similar securities.

The question now arises : which rate of interest shall we have in view in discussing the necessity and the probable future of interest? The answer is, of course, that a complete theory of interest must examine into the causes by which the price of each special form of waiting is governed. Still there seem to be strong reasons why we should concentrate our attention on " waiting for long periods." This form of waiting is, as has already been said, the real and principal form ; and a very considerable quantity of capital must be looked upon as invested under such conditions—specially if we consider how much capital is fixed in the capitalists' own undertakings. Accordingly, in the following discussion, by " the rate of interest " we shall mean the price of " waiting for long periods." When it is contended that the rate of interest probably will never sink below 1½ per cent., it is the long period rate that is referred to ; and it must be understood that nothing has been said about the price of waiting under more favourable conditions. For no one would deny that the price for " waiting on call " could temporarily go down to nil.

Lending money on first mortgage on real property

may be taken as a type of the kind of waiting we
have in view here.   There is practically no risk in
it ; the lender can get his money back again on
giving the stipulated notice, or he may transfer the
security to a third person ; only his security has not
the extra and artificial advantage of being introduced
on the Stock Exchange and dealt with there every
day.

The objection might be raised that there is a
certain amount of trouble and even expense in con-
tracting such a loan, and that, accordingly, since
the rate of interest obtainable in this way includes
remuneration for trouble, this operation does not
represent a pure and simple function of waiting.
This objection leads us to consider, more generally,
the question of "trouble" in connection with lending of money.   There is always some trouble connected with the arranging and carrying out of a
loan contract.   Supposing a middleman to take over
this trouble as a special function, we arrive at the
necessity of considering, as regards every loan, two
different rates of interest : one rate paid by the
borrower, and therefore governing the demand for
waiting, another and a lower rate paid to the lender
and therefore governing the supply of waiting.
The difference between the two rates, representing
the payment for "trouble," depends very much on
the organisation of the market for every particular
kind of security.   It seems to vary much even from
one country to another.   In Sweden, the banks
generally take charge of mortgage securities and
receive the interest on behalf of the lender at the
trifling annual commission of one half pro mille (one
shilling per cent.).   Deducting this quota from the
rate of interest, which varies between 4 and 5 per
cent., the rest may be said to represent, truly and
properly, the reward of waiting, the capitalist having
nothing more to do than to draw cheques on his bank.

§ 2. *Causes governing the Supply of Waiting.*

"The amount of net produce, this excess of production above the physical necessaries of the producers, is one of the elements that determine the amount of saving. The greater the produce of labour after supporting the labourers, the more there is which *can* be saved. The same thing also partly contributes to determine how much *will* be saved."[1]

In these remarks *Mill* has noted an important cause governing the supply of waiting, viz. the *capacity for saving*. It might be defined, more broadly, as the surplus of the produce of a society over and above the necessaries which such a society must consume in order to maintain its actual standard of efficiency. So much is, of course, never saved ; still this capacity for saving has a great bearing on its actual volume.

Impressed by the enormous growth of productivity of recent times, people have accustomed themselves to look on the possibility of creating capital as quite unlimited. This conclusion is however not quite consistent.

The productivity of society will certainly continue to increase. But at the same time the "necessaries of efficiency" will increase : firstly, because of the growth of population ; secondly, because of the rise in the labourers' standard of consumption, which is, to a great extent, a necessary condition of higher efficiency. The question then arises whether the productivity or the necessaries of efficiency are likely to increase faster. This is an extremely delicate question, involving among other things the old controversy as to the problem of population. It is, therefore, rather dangerous to contend—as is so often done—that the capacity for saving, which is

---

[1] *John Stuart Mill*, Principles of Political Economy, Book I., Ch. XI., § 1.

the difference between productivity and necessaries, must increase.

Further, increasing productivity is possible only under the condition of a corresponding increase of capital. Indeed, as we have seen in the preceding chapter, an increase of productivity will require in the future, not merely a proportional, but probably even a still greater increase in the use of capital. Thus an unlimited growth of productivity would imply an unlimited growth of capital. Hence there seems to be no reason for believing that the market will be better supplied with capital on the ground of an increasing productivity.

From these considerations a negative conclusion at least may be drawn : the common assumption that capital—or at least the capacity for creating capital—has a natural and necessary tendency to grow faster than the demand for it, is wholly unjustified.

To come now to the second chief factor in the supply of waiting, viz. the *desire of waiting*. The strength of this desire may be said generally to manifest itself in the relative degrees to which future and present needs are satisfied.

It has been pointed out by several writers how little is thought, in primitive societies, of any kind of provision for the future.[1] The principal reason given for this is the extreme insecurity which usually prevails in such societies, and, indeed, makes all kinds of disposition for the future uncertain. As security of property as well as of life increases, habits of prudence and forethought begin to develop. Some weight is now attached to future needs, and such needs are even provided for, so far as they do not interfere with the more urgent needs of the present. At higher stages of development, more

[1] Cf. e.g. *Rae*, New Principles of Political Economy, Book II., Ch. VI. ; and *Mill*, Book IV., Ch. IV., § 3.

and more distant needs are taken into consideration, and the relative importance attached to them increases.

Now this general tendency in the development of the human mind, may be regarded as a historical fact, and, arguing from it, some have been induced to contend that this development will go on in the same direction *ad infinitum*.

A little consideration, however, will show the groundlessness and the improbability of such a conclusion. The evolution in question may be described as a rise in the estimation put upon future needs as compared with the estimation put upon present ones. But such a rise obviously cannot go beyond a certain limit and must "slow down" very greatly as it nears this limit.

Present needs are necessarily more urgent than future ones. This should not be understood as meaning that every present need is more urgent than any future one. But if we compare two needs, each of which has the same importance in its own time, that one which is present is generally more urgent than that which belongs to the future. The most obvious reason for the greater importance of present needs is that present life is an indispensable condition for future life. The labourer must have his food to-day, otherwise next year's food would be of no use to him. Nor is this consideration confined to the maintenance of physical life. It is just as evident that the support of health, strength, and efficiency at the present time is, for every one, a necessary condition of being able to earn and enjoy anything in the future. The person who would deprive himself of every enjoyment for the present in order to save it for the future, would soon find that he had lost that mental activity and brightness without which no real enjoyment is possible. Again, the uncertainty of life makes it always doubtful whether a man will ever enjoy what he has saved for the future, even if he has invested it in first class securities. On such grounds present needs are generally, and rightly, regarded as more important than future ones.

Naturally these grounds for the under-estimation of future needs are strongest among those classes who are able to provide only very scantily even for the present. Indeed, the labourer would be a bad economist if he deprived himself of sufficient food in order to save for the future. But in the higher classes of wage earners more importance is attached to future needs. And in the middle and upper classes there is evidently a strong tendency to put future needs on the same level as present ones.

From this high estimation of future needs, it does not, however, necessarily follow that people will save. A man who attaches the same importance to future needs as to present ones, if he expects to be able to provide for his needs in the future just as easily as he does now, has no reason for setting aside anything of his present income; he is quite right in acting in accordance with the old saying : " every day has its own trouble." Now, this is the case with that large class who earn a fixed salary, and a salary which usually rises as the family expenses grow. It is also the case, even in a higher degree, with the capitalist living on the return from his capital, and also, though subject to more uncertainty, with the ordinary merchant or factory owner. What these classes have to do, in order to make the same provision for the future as for the present, is, first, to make their expected incomes in the future sure, and, second, to set aside a sum for a time when they will not be able to earn such incomes. By business men, these ends are largely attained through accumulating capital ; by the other classes concerned, mainly through the insurance policy, which serves as a protection against risks, and, at the same time, as a medium for accumulation.

On these grounds, a person who desires to provide for his future just as well as he provides for his present, has, as a rule, to save some minor part of his income. This much, however, is actually saved by great numbers of people. There seems little reason to assume that such persons will come to save more ; for this would mean that they attach *higher* importance to future than to present needs. Hence the possibility of a further growth of accumulation in this direction—with the object of providing for future needs—is limited to an extension of similar habits to the whole population, and specially to the great class of wage-earners. This will, however, be a slow process, and will obviously require a simultaneous rise in the whole standard of consumption of the labourer.

Nor is it very probable that further development will lead us to take more distant needs into consideration. People are already providing for their lifetime and for their children. More cannot reasonably be asked for. It would simply be absurd to consider and try to provide for the needs of our grandchildren or for still more distant generations. On this account we cannot expect any very considerable increase in the desire for waiting.

In this connection something should be said as to the investment of money in the education of children. From the parents' point of view such investment is equivalent to the accumulation of a certain amount of capital for the benefit of their children. The parents, then, may be said to supply a quantity of waiting ; but the children, who consume at an earlier period what they will earn only at a later, must in this case also be counted as demanders of the same quantity of waiting. We may, therefore, very well omit this whole item in our account of the demand

and supply of waiting.   Even the community, which
provides a certain amount of free education, may
be said to invest money ; undoubtedly it supplies a
certain amount of waiting ; but it seems better not
to count this supply, nor the children's demand for
it ; otherwise we should be tempted to count the
children themselves as capital, waiting being always
intimately connected with the use of capital.   Such
confusing terminology has sometimes been used, but
it should be avoided.

It might be said to be a general tendency of
modern life to sacrifice more and more for the sake
of education.   But this tendency gives no weight to
the supposition that the total desire of accumulation
is growing : it is immediately counterbalanced by the
demand for waiting arising from the children's consumption in anticipation of their future incomes.

Summing up our argument, we may state, in
conclusion, that, although the progress of civilisation
has been marked hitherto by a continuous growth
in the desire of providing for future needs, it would
be wrong to assume that this growth is unlimited.

Curiously enough, however, there seems to be
another reason for saving, which cannot properly be
accounted for as a desire of providing for future
needs.   When a great capitalist with an annual
income of, say, £100,000, accepts a certain standard
of life requiring £30,000 of yearly expenses, and
thus saves £70,000 a year, and has the intention
of going on doing so, he cannot be said to provide
for future needs.   He simply accumulates capital for
the sake of accumulation.   There may be various
reasons for doing this ; pure vanity and a desire to
rise in the estimation of what is called "society" ;
the demand of the born leader of industry to direct,
to govern, and to have a field of work large enough
for his activity and energy ; the obvious impossibility
of finding any reasonable way of spending the whole

of a great income ; the miser's senseless enjoyment of seeing himself "worth" so many thousands
or millions. But, whatever the reason, such accumulators of capital undoubtedly fulfil the social
function of waiting ; and this on the whole may
be of greater advantage to society than if these
wealthy individuals chose to spend their money.

Now we might ask whether such supply of
waiting has a tendency to increase or to decline ;
but it seems impossible to give a definite answer
to this question. It is evident, however, that the
luxury prevailing among the very rich is increasing ;
and this tendency must of course, other things being
equal, diminish their supply of waiting.

So much for the general tendencies prevailing in
regard to the desire of waiting. We have now to
examine a question of a more special character, but
of the highest importance for our problem, viz. the
influence of the rate of interest on the desire of
waiting.

The views of economists on this matter have
altered very much. It has been contended that a
high rate of interest would encourage the desire of
waiting, just as a high price generally brings out
supply ; and that, accordingly, capital must increase
faster when the rate of interest is high. On the
other hand, it has been emphasised that persons
desiring to procure for themselves a certain annual
income are compelled to accumulate a much larger
capital if the rate of interest is low.

In order to clear up these points, it is necessary to
distinguish, as we have done above, between the
different classes of accumulators. The great capitalist,
who has adopted a certain standard of life and who
has accustomed himself to set aside the rest of his
income whatever it may be, would surely save less
were his income considerably diminished by a serious
fall in the rate of interest. As this class of accumu-

lators at the present time account for a large part of
the total supply of waiting, there can be no doubt that
such a decrease in their savings would make itself
felt.   It is true that certain incomes of the capitalist
class have the character of rents fixed for a longer
or shorter time.   In so far as this is the case, the
effect of a fall in the rate of interest would be
retarded.

The better class labourers, who now accumulate a
small capital as a kind of insurance fund against
lack of employment, sickness, and so on, would
probably act in the same manner whatever the rate
of interest.   As a fact, the accumulations of the
savings banks have shown themselves to be very
little affected by the rate.   Almost the same might
be said of the accumulation of capital now made
through the medium of insurance companies, though
it seems probable that the higher premiums which
would result from a lower rate of interest would
for some time put a check on such business.

As regards the great class of accumulators who
aim at acquiring a capital large enough to enable
them to live on the interest, the matter is more
complicated.   Such a capital may be accumulated in
many different ways.   It can be done by a relatively
small annual sacrifice provided that the accumulation
is extended over a long period ; or it can be done
in a shorter time but at a larger annual cost.   It is
necessary, however, in order to elucidate the question
to discuss a special case ; this should be chosen so
as to represent, so far as possible, normal conditions.

There must, generally, be some reasonable proportion between sacrifice and end, between the
annual savings and the future income they are
intended to assure.   A proportion of one to one
seems rather large, and it is probable that in most
cases people do not sacrifice so much for the future.
There is a strong desire among most people that

their future income should not fall short of their present living expenses. But the annual saving of a sum equal to these expenses means a saving of one half the current income, which must be regarded as a very high degree of parsimony. Even if people content themselves with a future income equal to the half of their present expenses, the annual saving of such a sum requires the saving of a third of current incomes, which still involves a considerable sacrifice. We may conclude therefore that most people are not prepared to save annually a larger sum than that which they intend to provide for themselves as future annual income.

Let us suppose, then, that a person has decided to provide for himself a future income of £1,000, but that he is not prepared, under any circumstances, to set aside more than this same sum of £1,000 a year. If the rate of interest is 6 per cent., he may easily attain his end by accumulating a capital which affords him the desired income. Such capital need not be more than $16\frac{2}{3}$ times as large as his annual savings. But if the rate falls the task will be more and more difficult. At 3 per cent. he must accumulate $33\frac{1}{3}$ times as much as his annual savings ; at $1\frac{1}{2}$ per cent, $66\frac{2}{3}$ times as much. We see now where the difficulty arises. *The shortness of the active period of human life* must, sooner or later, if the rate of interest is supposed steadily to fall, absolutely prohibit any attempt to accumulate a capital sufficient to yield an income equal to the sum annually saved or even anything like it. In fact, actual calculation shows that the time required for such a purpose is :

At a rate of interest of	6 per cent.	. . .	12 years.
,, ,, ,,	3 ,,	. . .	24 ,,
,, ,, ,,	2 ,,	. . .	35 ,,
,, ,, ,,	$1\frac{1}{2}$,,	. . .	47 ,,
,, ,, ,,	1 ,,	. . .	70 ,,

These figures give us at once the correct view of the problem before us. If the rate of interest fall from 6 per cent. to about 3 per cent., people will adhere to the method formerly adopted for procuring a future income, viz., the accumulation of capital ; it will cost them more effort, but still it will be possible. This will have the effect of making them, individually, accumulate much larger capitals,—in the special case assumed, twice as much. Consequently, the effect of the fall in the rate is an increase in the supply of waiting and a very considerable increase. This is what those writers have had in view who have emphasised that a low rate must force people to save more.

But if the rate of interest continues to fall and reaches such a point as $1\frac{1}{2}$ per cent., the effect upon the supply of waiting will be just the reverse. People will no longer see their way to provide the income desired by the method of accumulating capital. They will accordingly abandon it, and adopt another method which will serve the main purpose just as well, but will not give the additional satisfaction of possessing a certain capital. Such a revolution in the conduct of large numbers could not fail to very seriously affect the total supply of waiting.

We arrive at the same result if we start from another standpoint. Assuming that a man of the class we are speaking of is able on an average to go on accumulating for 25 years (which is rather long, as people do not generally arrive at large incomes at an early age), he may attempt to accumulate a capital yielding the desired income by saving a certain sum annually during the 25 years. But this sum will, at various rates of interest, bear the following proportions to the income which the accumulator desires to procure for himself :

At a rate of interest of 6 per cent. . . . 0·30
    ,,   ,,   ,.   3 ,,   . . . 0·91

At a rate of interest of 2 per cent. . . . 1·6
  ,,   ,,   ,, $1\frac{1}{2}$,, . . . 2·2
  ,,   ,,   ,, 1 ,, . . . 3·6

It is clear that there will be, even at a rate of 3 per cent., a strong temptation to many people to give up the task and to adopt an easier scheme of providing for the future. And this will be done on a very large scale if the rate goes down below 2 per cent.

It follows from what has now been said that, with a rate of interest of something like $1\frac{1}{2}$ per cent., all forces would combine in weakening very considerably the desire of accumulation in the very classes which now contribute the largest part of the total supply of waiting.

But a very low rate of interest would have another and an additional effect ; namely, that small capitalists would begin, very generally, to consume their capital. This is a matter of the utmost importance for the theory of interest, and we shall therefore consider it more in detail.

It is clear, to begin with, that a capitalist cannot consume his capital in the literal sense of the word. But he may retain the whole or a part of his money when it is paid back, or he may find a third person willing to take over his function of waiting. People who, in this sense, consume their capital, obviously withdraw a part of the total amount of waiting already supplied. If such a practice became general, it would have quite a disastrous effect.

Let us therefore analyse what influence a fall in the rate of interest would have on the tendency to consume capital. The most rational way in which a person may consume his capital is that of buying an annuity for the rest of his life. Whether he will do this or not, depends of course very much on the proportion in which his annual income will thereby be increased. This, again, depends partly

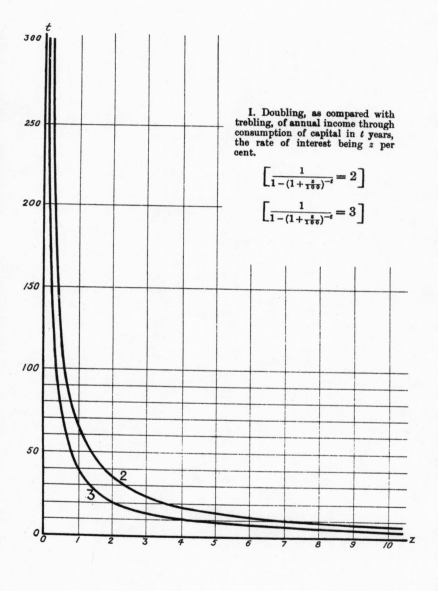

I. Doubling, as compared with trebling, of annual income through consumption of capital in t years, the rate of interest being z per cent.

$$\left[\frac{1}{1-(1+\tfrac{z}{100})^{-t}} = 2\right]$$

$$\left[\frac{1}{1-(1+\tfrac{z}{100})^{-t}} = 3\right]$$

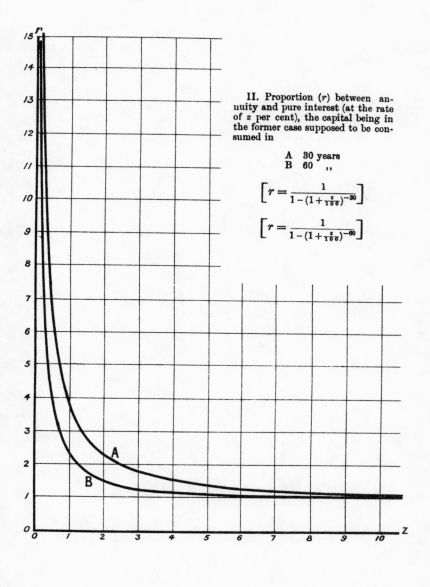

II. Proportion (r) between annuity and pure interest (at the rate of z per cent), the capital being in the former case supposed to be consumed in

A   30 years
B   60 ,,

$$\left[r = \frac{1}{1-(1+\frac{z}{100})^{-30}} \right]$$

$$\left[r = \frac{1}{1-(1+\frac{z}{100})^{-60}} \right]$$

on the length of the period during which he will consume his capital, and partly on the rate of interest. Let us suppose, in order to fix our thoughts, that a capitalist, in such a position that he can independently dispose of his capital, has on an average 30 years more to live. Then, if the rate of interest is high, he will not gain very much by exchanging his interest-income for an annuity ; but if the rate of interest falls below 2 per cent., the gain becomes substantial, and the capitalist will readily be induced to consume his capital. Again, supposing the capitalist willing even to provide an income for his children, he might have the choice between simple interest on his capital and an annuity for sixty years. The advantage of the annuity scheme is purely nominal with an ordinary rate of interest ; but becomes considerable at a rate of $1\frac{1}{2}$ per cent., and quite overwhelming at a lower rate.

The whole matter is best illustrated by the following table, where the proportion between annuity and interest is given for different rates of interest, under the assumption that the capital is consumed in 30 and 60 years.

Rate of interest.	Capital consumed in 30 years.	Capital consumed in 60 years.
$\frac{1}{4}$	13·9	7·19
$\frac{1}{2}$	7·20	3·87
$\frac{3}{4}$	4·98	2·77
1	3·87	2·22
$1\frac{1}{2}$	2·78	1·69
2	2·23	1·44
3	1·70	1·20
4	1·45	1·11
5	1·30	1·06
6	1·21	1·03
10	1·06	1·003

A glance at this table is sufficient to make it clear that the gap between 2 per cent. and 1 per cent. is

very critical, and that the rate of interest cannot
pass through it without forcing a great number of
capitalists to begin consuming their capital.   The
table will besides, it is hoped, give every one a
vivid impression of the absurdity of the supposition
that the rate of interest could ever sink to a fraction
of 1 per cent.

It is obvious that an opportunity of doubling, and
still more of trebling, an insufficient interest-income
must be a very strong inducement to set aside considerations of minor importance, such as the leaving
of one's capital intact for the benefit of more or less
distant relatives.   It is, of course, possible, at every
rate of interest, to double or even treble the income
drawn from capital, if only the period of consumption
be sufficiently short.   The higher the rate of interest,
the more must this period be reduced.   At the
ordinary rate of interest of, say, 4 per cent., it is
possible to double the income by consuming the
capital in 17·7 years, and to treble it by consuming
the capital in 10·3 years.   Supposing the rate to be
3 per cent., the corresponding figures are 23·4 and
13·7 years.   Accordingly, experience shows that the
majority of those who buy annuities are between
60 and 70 years of age.   But if the rate went down
to 2 per cent., it would be possible to draw¦ double
the income in the form of an annuity for 35 years,
which period would cover the remainder of life for
most adults.   And, at 1 per cent., everyone would
be able to treble his income for the rest of his life at
the cost of not leaving anything behind him.   It
can hardly be doubted that, under such circumstances, a very considerable part of the present
supply of waiting would be withdrawn.

The following table gives the number of years
for which a capital would last, when gradually consumed so as to provide an income respectively two
and three times as large as the interest.

Rate of interest.	Double income.	Treble income.
$\frac{1}{4}$	277·6	162·3
$\frac{1}{2}$	139·0	81·3
$\frac{3}{4}$	92·8	54·3
1	69·7	40·7
$1\frac{1}{2}$	46·6	27·2
2	35·0	20·5
3	23·4	13·7
4	17·7	10·3
5	14·2	8·3
6	11·9	7·0
10	7·3	4·3

This table also makes it clear that the gap between 2 per cent. and 1 per cent. is a critical one. Above 2 per cent. an income can hardly be doubled and still less trebled—if the capital is to last to the end of life—unless in the case of old people. But, below 1 per cent., income can be trebled and still the capital will last for periods covering the life not only of one generation but also of the next. There would, under such circumstances, be no reason why capitalists should abstain from consuming their capital.

" The number of years' purchase for which a fixed annual rent will sell " is only another expression for the rate of interest; supposing the rate to be 4 per cent. or $\frac{1}{25}$, the number of years' purchase is 25. This mode of expressing the matter has great advantages. For it is obvious that no one will offer a number of years' purchase greater than the number of years for which he intends to provide. It is perhaps not apparent to everyone that there is something natural in a rate of interest of 3 or 4 per cent. But it is quite obvious that the number of years' purchase for which the same nominal rental will sell in the market must tend to be something between 25 and $33\frac{1}{3}$ years, and is not likely to surpass the latter limit, for the simple reason that human life is short.

There is, in fact, an intimate connection between the average length of human life and the rate of interest. In a state of war, of internal disorders or general insecurity in regard to life, or in bad climates, the probable length of life is short, and the rate of interest has always, under such circumstances, been high. Though other forces have, certainly, contributed to that result, it cannot be doubted that the shortness of life has been an essential cause. On the other hand, " were life to endure for ever" and "were we guided solely by the dictates of reason, there could be no limit to the formation of means for future gratification."[1] In other words, a substantial increase in the average length of life would in all probability be followed by a fall of the rate of interest. But people who predict that the rate of interest will altogether disappear seem scarcely more reasonable than the old English socialist *Godwin*, who earnestly asked why we should not, one day, become immortal!

§ 3. *Conclusions.*

Among modern writers on economics we very often find the idea expressed that interest may, and probably will, sink to a very low rate or even become negative. It is conceivable, we are told, that savings may increase "until the accumulation of capital reaches such a point that interest becomes nominal, or even negative." . . . "It is a distinct advantage to those who wish to make future provision to have wealth kept for them until such time as it is most convenient to consume it," . . . "and in case of a glut of capital for industrial purposes, it might be necessary to pay for this employment, just as you pay an agent for farming land in hand,

[1] *Rae*, New Principles of Political Economy, Book II. Ch. VI.

or a caretaker for living in an unlet house." [1]   Certainly it might be in exceptional cases,—from which, however, we cannot draw the conclusion that the market rate of interest may become negative, any more than we might conclude, from the case of the caretaker, that there might come a time when house-rent generally would be paid by the owners to the occupiers !

It is a common belief that the rate of interest has a natural tendency to fall ; from the alleged fact that it has fallen hitherto, it is concluded that it will continue to do so for the future.   Both the fact and the conclusion are extremely doubtful.   It is to be remembered that we have been discussing only the market rate ; therefore, we cannot go back in our comparisons to times when no market yet existed ; and, in times when interest was severely prohibited, no market can be said to have existed.   The first real market for the use of capital is perhaps to be found in Holland in the middle of the seventeenth century, when the usual rate is said to have been

---

[1] *Foxwell*, The Social Aspect of Banking.   Journal of the Institute of Bankers.   Vol. VII., 1886.   This is only one instance out of hundreds.   Leading economists in almost all countries could be quoted in support of similar views.   In a note to his chapter on "Interest of Capital" (Principles of Economics, Book VI., Ch. VI., § I.), Professor *Marshall* points out "how small a modification of the conditions of our own world would be required to bring us to another in which the mass of the people are so anxious to provide for old age and for their families after them, and in which the new openings for the advantageous use of accumulated wealth in any form are so small, that the amount of wealth for the safe custody of which people are willing to pay exceeds that which others desire to borrow; and where in consequence even those who saw their way to make a gain out of the use of capital, would be able to exact a payment for taking charge of it ; and interest would be negative all along the line."—This note excellently serves the purpose of emphasising that interest is a price governed like all other prices exclusively by demand and supply ; but, as it stands, it is apt to give support to essentially erroneous ideas about the market for waiting.

about 3 per cent. The shares of the Dutch East-Indian Company did not, in the period anterior to the French Revolution, pay more than $2\frac{3}{4}$ per cent. on their usual price ; and the provincial $2\frac{1}{2}$ per cent. debenture stocks were quoted at par or even above. In England 3 per cent. was a common rate for good securities in the time of George II. In fact, the rate of interest is not lower to-day in the leading countries of the world than it often was, one or two centuries ago, in Holland, in England, in the sea-ports of Spain, or in the principal commercial centres of Germany.[1]

But even if the rate of interest had shown, during the past two centuries, a decided tendency to fall, this would not justify the conclusion that the rate must fall still further. Every such conclusion would be entirely unscientific. Granted that a curve has fallen within a certain interval, this is no reason why it should not rise again or take a horizontal course. The latter seems most probable in the case of interest. Economic and social progress has brought interest down to between 4 and 3 per cent.; there are reasons for believing that the rate will not, in the future, go very much below that point, nor yet, for any considerable time, rise much above it.

We may now endeavour to strike the balance of the different tendencies influencing the demand and the supply of waiting. The principal tendency on the supply side, in fact the only one which has more than a very limited range, is the growth of social productivity and the consequent growth of the capacity for saving. But the higher productivity is, to a large extent, counterbalanced by the greater consumption resulting from the growth of population

---

[1] Cf. *Roscher*, Principles of Political Economy ; *Leroy-Beaulieu*, De la répartition des richesses, Paris, 1888 ; and *d'Aulnuis de Bourouill*, Der Zinsfuss. Die Ursachen seines Sinkens und seine nächste Zukunft. *Conrad's* Jahrbücher, Band 52.

and of individual "necessaries of efficiency." Increasing productivity cannot, therefore, be taken as
proof of a corresponding increase of the capacity
for saving. Still it seems probable that there will
for a long time to come, be some increase in the
capacity for saving. But then we must remember
that the growth of productivity entirely depends on
a rapidly increasing supply of capital, the principal
mark of progress being substitution of the use of
capital for other factors of production. The growth
of productivity might, therefore, very well absorb
the whole capacity of saving to which it gives rise,
and in itself, consequently, is no sufficient reason
for the conclusion, so often drawn from it, that
capital must some time become abundant.

The second tendency increasing the supply of
capital is the growth of the desire of saving. There
has, no doubt, been a very remarkable growth of
this desire throughout the whole historical development of society. But this tendency has its natural
limit : it is best characterised as a rising estimation
of future needs in comparison with that of present
needs, and must therefore necessarily come to a stop
when future needs have reached the same level of
estimation with present ones. We are already, as
shown above, near to such a state of things, and
cannot, therefore, expect great results from the
future development of this tendency. It is, besides,
to some extent, counterbalanced by an analogous
tendency on the demand side, namely, the growing
taste for durable goods, especially for houses and
furniture.

We have seen that the fall of the rate of interest,
say from 6 to 3 per cent., must have weakened the
desire of saving in some people, while stimulat-
ing it in others. It is therefore reasonable to
assume that it has had no very considerable effect
on the actual accumulation of capital. In a broad

sense it might be said that capital is just as willingly supplied at 3 per cent. as at 6. If this is so, it seems quite unreasonable to charge the capitalist with extorting interest from the rest of the community and thereby depriving the labourer of a part of the whole produce of his labour. In fact, capitalists have very little influence on the rate of interest ; they do not combine in order to raise the rate artificially ; they are even, as a class, quite prepared to take a somewhat lower rate than that current, and still supply the same amount of capital. The real cause which at the present time actually governs the rate of interest is the demand for the use of capital ; it is this demand that makes it necessary to charge the actual rate : at a lower rate the demand would immediately exceed the supply.

But it would be so no longer if the rate of interest went down considerably below 3 per cent. For it is tolerably certain that the suppliers of waiting, or the " capitalists," would then begin to react against the fall of the rate by withdrawing a part of their supply ; while the demand for waiting would at the same time be enormously stimulated. Thus the rate of interest could hardly fail to rise again.

Hence we may say in conclusion, that there is no reason for assuming that the rate of interest will sink in the future below the lowest level which it has reached hitherto on any great market.

If we have been compelled, for obvious reasons, to put this statement in a cautious and negative form, we may now state in more decided terms the second point in these conclusions, viz., that the rate of interest will never sink below $1\frac{1}{2}$ per cent. The reasons for this prediction are the same as those quoted above, only that they act, in this case, with incomparably greater force. A rate of

$1\frac{1}{2}$ per cent. would open an extremely large field for profitable investment of capital ; and would, at the same time, very seriously reduce the desire of accumulation and encourage the consumption of capital. Such a rate, therefore, if once reached, could not possibly signify a point of economic equilibrium. For instance, it is quite clear that the supposed consumption of capital could never take place : the first attempt at such a consumption on a large scale would immediately cause the market to collapse and force the rate to rise rapidly.

Finally, the same considerations, if only followed out with logical severity, will reveal the evident absurdity of the assumption that interest may at some time or other be altogether dispensed with. Thus the main argument of this book, viz., the necessity of interest, is established, so far, at least, as the present individualistic society is concerned.

CHAPTER V

§ 1. *Methods of Securing Stability for the Money Standard.*

In the preceding chapters we have considered money merely as a sort of scale by which people may conveniently express their estimation of different commodities and services. As a fact, the principal function of money is to serve as such a scale. Material money is besides used as a means of exchange, and is sometimes hoarded. But neither of these uses is of any primary importance for us in working out a general theory of prices. It should also be observed that, in practice, every money system is in the first place a scale of measurement, coins being only one of many different tools for the purpose of sale and purchase, all of them deriving their purchasing power from the recognition given them as representing money.

Such a money scale, however, always contains one arbitrary element; for as all estimates are necessarily relative to one another, their expressions in money may be all multiplied by one constant factor. Now, if that factor were allowed to vary from time to time, estimates at different periods could not be compared with one another—at least not directly; and, as it is of great practical import-ance that the price-scale should not be liable to such variations, different methods have been adopted, or proposed, in order to secure a certain stability for the money standard.

The scheme commonly adopted in order to bring about this result, consists in fixing the price for one single article. Generally indeed the price is not absolutely fixed ; but is allowed to vary between certain limits which should be drawn as close to each other as possible.

Evidently this method would answer its purpose perfectly if there were no variations in the relative prices of different commodities. But as such variations always take place the method is necessarily more or less defective.

The article whose price is fixed in this way is generally gold or silver. The present money standard of England might be described as a Pound Sterling standard, all payments being made in pounds sterling. But, in order to secure a certain stability for this standard, the price of gold has been fixed ; it is not absolutely fixed indeed, but provisions are made to prevent the price of gold rising above one certain point or sinking below another. This lower point is absolutely fixed, and is £3 17s. 9d. per ounce standard weight (11 parts gold, 1 part alloy), the Bank of England immediately paying that sum to the depositor of gold. The upper limit of the gold price is not so absolutely fixed. If the demand for gold has to be satisfied out of the circulating coin, the price will depend on the quality of this coin. Theoretically, the standard ounce should be contained in £3 17s. 10½d., and this therefore should be the upper limit of the gold price. But this is a purely ideal figure. The remedy, or the tolerated variation from the exact standard either of weight or of fineness of coins issued from the Mint, would allow the gold price to rise considerably higher ; but as the sovereign is struck with much greater exactness than that required by law, this kind of variation has no great importance. If, however, the gold coins were allowed to become worn, the gold price might rise very seriously ; hence light coins have to be withdrawn and replaced by new ones. Modern Coinage Acts generally make some provision for this purpose. But as the actual maximum price of gold depends on the average condition of the circulating medium, it follows that this maximum point is not determined absolutely. If the central bank specially supplies gold for export, the upper limit of the gold price depends on the policy of the bank. The Bank of France usually sells standard gold only at a premium, thus enlarging the margin for the variations of the gold price—a policy which seems to be in contradiction with the very purpose of securing stability for the monetary standard.

Bimetallism might, from the present point of view, be described as an attempt to secure a stable money standard through fixing the prices of *two* articles, gold and silver. This, however, involves a difficulty, not to say an impossibility, and this difficulty has no immediate connection with the problem of preventing the variations of the standard, viz., the fixing of the proportion between the prices of two different articles.

The socialistic programme, claiming for the labourer "the whole produce of his labour," includes the creation of what has been called "labour money." In this case "labour" is chosen as the article whose price is to be fixed in order to secure stability to the general scale of prices ; it is obviously quite irrelevant whether the standard unit in such a system is called "normal hour," mark, crown, or anything else.

Instead of fixing the price of a single article, we

could of course select a number of articles, make
some sort of a mean of their prices, and fix this
mean-price. That is, in fact, the method of those
who advocate a standard based on an index-
number. We should perhaps in this way secure a
higher stability for our money scale than is attain-
able by fixing the price of a single article. But we
need not expect to reach perfection in matters like
this. It is impossible even to give a strict definition of what we wish to attain. We might say the
aim is that there should be no variations of prices
due to variations of the standard ; but we do not
know precisely how to ascertain such variations.
We have only that somewhat rough and ready test
derived from the principle that variations of the
standard must affect all prices in the same direction.
However, as prices always vary in relation to one
another, there is never a simple and clear variation
of all prices in the same direction. We must content
ourselves, then, with observing the movements of
"the general level of prices." But here again we
find that such a level admits of no strict definition.

Let us, however, return to the consideration of the
actual standard of our time. The fixing of two
limits for the variation of the price of gold is a
guide, but is not, properly speaking, a means for
securing stability to the money scale. It is, for
instance, not enough for the law to enact that the
price of gold shall never exceed a certain sum.
Some measures must be taken in order to secure
effectively that it shall not do so. This is generally
brought about by the central bank holding a stock
of gold, sufficiently large to guarantee that the bank
shall always be able to sell gold at the fixed
maximum price, and to any amount required. This
however, would never be possible, if the bank did
not take some other measure in order to protect its
gold reserve. This ultimate measure, on which the

maintenance of the approximately fixed gold price depends, is, as is well known, the discount policy of the bank.

We may ask, then, if a sufficient stability of the money scale could not be maintained without imposing any regulation as to the price of some single article or some group of articles. What would happen if the money scale were left free from all such restrictions? The answer is that the central bank, trusted with the control of the standard, would perhaps lend too much money to the public. This would stimulate investment of money and creation of capital, *i.e.* the productive forces of the society would be directed in an undue degree to future ends. Thus, the supply of present goods being comparatively scanty, and buyers at the same time numerous and abundantly supplied with money, prices could not fail to rise. Or the bank would lend too little to the public, and the very opposite effects would follow.

Hence we see that the problem of securing stability to the money scale is essentially a question of the regulation of credit.

It is conceivable that the bank might keep the proper middle course and lend just so much as not to influence prices in one direction or the other. This is exactly what the bank should do ; and, if it could be trusted always to follow such a policy, no special regulations would be necessary. We may say, too, that the present fixing of certain limits for the gold price, and other similar regulations, have no other purpose than to compel the bank to observe a credit policy which will insure stability of prices ; and certainly the possibility must be admitted that a higher degree of stability might be attained without such regulations.

Now it is universally accepted that credit can be regulated efficiently by the single expedient of the rate of interest, and, indeed, that it should not be interfered with in any other manner. Hence all schemes for securing stability of money, though they differ considerably in the means they propose to use, ultimately depend on the same expedient—a wise administration of the bank-rate.

§ 2. *Appreciation and Interest.*

Before proceeding further, we must clear up the purely arithmetical relations between Appreciation and Interest. This part of the problem presents no difficulties; it is indeed of very much the same nature as the ordinary corrections of thermometers, and other physical instruments, for dilatation of the scale.[1]

If the prices of all commodities advance, say 2 per cent., we shall say that the monetary standard has been *depreciated* 2 per cent. in regard to an ideal, invariable standard. Similarly, if the prices of commodities fall 2 per cent., we shall say that the actual standard has *appreciated* 2 per cent. in regard to the ideal standard. If there is an appreciation of 2 per cent. per year we shall say that the *rate of appreciation* is 0·02. Generally, we shall denote the rate of appreciation by s. The same sign will be used to denote the rate of depreciation, only that in this case s is understood to be negative.

A sum of money, let us call it K, which constantly appreciates at the rate s, is every year multiplied by the factor $1 + s$, which we shall denote by q. Consequently, after a number of years equal to t, the original sum K is worth in the ideal standard $K.q^t$. The formula is the same in the case of depreciation. The whole phenomenon of appreciation or deprecia-

---

[1] The problem has been thoroughly studied by *Fisher* in his able paper on "Appreciation and Interest." Publications of the American Economic Association, 1896.

tion may therefore, from a purely arithmetical point of view, be described as a multiplication by a certain factor, q.

Now, as everybody knows, the same applies to the growth of a capital to which interest is yearly added. If r is the rate of interest, and if $p = 1 + r$, a capital, K, will, after t years, become $K.p^t$. The capital is simply multiplied at the end of every year by the factor p.

Hence a sum of money K which bears interest at the rate r and at the same time appreciates at the rate s, is every year multiplied by the factor $p.q$. This compound phenomenon, therefore, has the same arithmetical character as any of the simple ones of which it is made up. Denoting $p.q$ by P, and putting $P = 1 + R$, we may represent R as the *real* rate of interest paid, whilst r is the *contract* rate. As

$$P = p\, q,$$

we have

$$R = r + s + rs.$$

Both r and s being generally small fractions, we may, without considerable error, omit the term rs, which seldom amounts to 0·001. We thus arrive at the simple approximate rule that the real rate of interest is equal to the contract rate, augmented by the rate of appreciation or diminished by the rate of depreciation. Thus, it is always possible, at the end of a loan, when the rate of appreciation or depreciation becomes known, to calculate the real rate of interest. Supposing the contract rate to have been agreed upon under the assumption that there will be no variation in the money-standard, the borrower suffers a loss of capital in the case of appreciation, but makes a gain of capital in the case of depreciation. This loss or gain however may always, and should most conveniently be, accounted for as too high or too low a rate of interest, *i.e.* as a deviation of the contract rate of interest from what should have been agreed upon had the future variation of the standard been anticipated.

It is also evident that, if everybody thoroughly realised that there would be, in the future, a general fall of prices, the market rate of interest would be equal to the rate that would prevail in the same market were no variation of the standard anticipated —diminished by the rate of the future appreciation. In terms of our formula : the contract rate r would be equal to the real rate R, diminished by the rate of appreciation s, or $r = R - s$. By accepting such a lower nominal rate, both parties in fact agree upon a real rate in accordance with the conditions of the market for the use of capital.

The question whether people do in reality take account of future variations of the money standard, when entering on loan-contracts, or to what extent they do so, is a very delicate one, and cannot be dealt with here. Of course every manufacturer or merchant, who anticipates a rise of prices in those special articles with which he deals, is anxious to borrow money in order to extend his business and thus take advantage of the rise. In this sense it may be said that an anticipation of a rise in prices always has an influence on the rate of interest. But, on the other hand, it seems quite certain that no investor of capital takes account of the possibility that his money may be worth less to him when he gets it back. We may therefore regard the market rate of interest as a true expression of what the ordinary saver expects to get. And the total amount of waiting supplied must represent very nearly the supply which would be called forth were the nominal market rate also a real rate.

Thus the fact that money-lenders sometimes ultimately find they have received a very low real rate of interest, does not prove that they would have willingly accepted this low rate. This result justifies the conclusion we have drawn in the foregoing from observations of the more or less nominal rate of the market.

The connections, which we have now found to exist, between interest and appreciation make it evident that we can never arrive at an accurate explanation of the pure phenomenon of interest without excluding in some way all variations of the money standard.

§ 3. *The true problem of Interest.*

Interest may, from a certain point of view, be regarded as an agio paid for present goods in exchange for future ones. We have shown in the preceding chapter that there must necessarily be, in the market, such an underestimation of future goods in general. But, if we consider a special commodity, it is by no means certain that a definite quantity of that commodity would always be estimated more highly if supplied now than if supplied at some future time. Take, for instance, eggs. In July everyone would pay more for a score of eggs to be delivered fresh after six months than for the same eggs to be delivered immediately. Something similar may frequently be observed in the quotations of the produce exchange.

It is only when we take all goods together that the underestimation of future goods becomes the rule. The agio which is then paid for present goods is to be regarded as the resultant of the estimates of all sorts of goods. Though some of these estimates go in quite the opposite direction, the rest of them have such an overwhelming influence that the resultant estimate of "goods in general" is to the advantage of present goods.

Hence it is seen that the whole conception of

interest has a definite meaning only in regard to
"goods in general." That is to say, a general comparison between the estimation of future and present
goods can be made only by means of a standard
commodity representing, and representing truly so
far as possible, all goods. Money is such a standard
commodity, but only under the condition that the
general level of prices is kept invariable. Hence
the true problem of interest can be studied only
where a stable money standard has been established.

The "use of capital," for which interest is paid, is
not the use of a piece of concrete capital, such as a
house, a machine, or a quantity of pig-iron, but is
the use of a certain amount of "goods in general."
This factor of production, therefore, cannot be
strictly defined unless we have some representative
for what is called "goods in general." An invariable
money standard affords such a representative, and
therefore also the ground for the definition we have
given of the "use of capital," viz., "the use of a
certain amount of money during a certain time."

Similarly in the case of "waiting." The pure
and obvious service of waiting is performed when
the same is paid back as has been lent; therefore,
if the thing lent is not a concrete piece of capital, but
"the command of a certain amount of goods in
general," the command of the same amount must be
paid back. This can, however, be secured only by
means of an invariable money-standard.

Now the fundamental means of securing stability
to the money-standard is, as shown above, the
regulation of the discount rate by the central banks
trusted with the control of the standard. Hence it
follows that the problem of interest presents itself,
in its true and genuine form, only in a society where
such a discount policy is pursued as will keep the
general price-level at a constant height. In such a
state of things, the rate of interest for every other

form of loan must adjust itself according to the movements of the discount-rate. Thus we arrive at the conclusion that *the true rate of interest, for any form of loan, is that which is necessary in order to prevent variations of the general price level, or, in other words, of the money standard.*

Supposing industry has been strongly stimulated, for instance, by a new invention or by the opening up of a new country, much fresh capital will be required in some branches of production, because they promise to yield a profit considerably above the rate of interest which has prevailed hitherto. This demand for the use of capital must be satisfied. But supposing the supply of fresh capital does not exceed the normal amount, it will evidently be necessary to check the use of capital in some of those purposes for which it could have been used under normal conditions. This will be done by increasing the rate of interest. For the function of the rate of interest, like that of all other prices, is to cut off such less urgent demand as cannot be satisfied, and to stimulate the supply. [In respect to an increase in the supply of waiting, not much, as we have seen, can be done by the usual variations of the rate.] With a higher rate of interest, the fresh capital coming on the market is reserved for such uses as promise to yield at least this higher rate ; in this way the available capital can be made to answer the demand. But if this splendid instrument, the rate of interest, is not properly used, if the banks go on giving credit at the old rate, the whole production of the community may be directed to future ends to a much greater extent than it would really desire. Under such circumstances, the supply of present goods cannot be made to meet the demand unless something artificial is done to restrain this demand ; that is, unless a general rise in the prices of commodities takes place.

It is probable also that this rise of prices will largely prevent those uses of capital which would otherwise, and more properly, have been prevented by a rise in the rate of interest. Thus a community may, by quoting a lower rate of interest than the market for the use of capital really requires, deceive itself ; but it would not gain any advantage thereby ; on the contrary, the rational direction of social production would invariably suffer from such a false policy.

The problem thus sketched may be called the *dynamic problem of interest*. It is in itself a very complicated problem and cannot even be defined in absolutely accurate terms, the conception of a price level being necessarily somewhat vague. It seems therefore highly desirable to state the problem of interest in a simpler and more exact form, even at the risk of sacrificing part of that concrete reality which the theory has to explain. We might do away with all difficulties arising from variations of prices by supposing *all* prices to be constant. We should then have to study the *static problem of interest* as a part of the general problem of equilibrium of prices. Supposing a state of equilibrium to have been established for a moment, we have to find the conditions which must be fulfilled in order that this equilibrium shall continue to the end of a certain period. An inquiry into these conditions must evidently clear up the nature of the different forces which tend every moment to alter prices ; that is to say, the forces which determine prices. Interest being one of those prices, the principal causes governing the rate of interest may be examined in this way.

Obviously all economic goods existing at the beginning of the period will have to be regarded as given factors of the problem. In so far as these goods are required for further production, they must be counted as independent factors of production. In particular, all concrete capital existing at the beginning of the period belongs to this category. This gives a very simple answer to the question how far back the process of production should be traced;—a question which has caused much confusion in *Böhm-Bawerk's* theory of interest. As it is clearly impossible to examine at once all the causes which have, from the beginning of the world, led to a certain result, all investigations of economic life should be strictly limited to a definite period. Every effect should be traced back to the beginning of this period, but that which exists at this moment belongs to the given factors of the problem. How the goods, and particularly the concrete capital, existing at the starting point, have been created or how much they might have cost, is of no importance : they are all on the same line with land which has not been produced by man, and therefore has not cost anything. The principal factors of production which must be supplied continuously in the production process are, as we have seen, labour, in the broadest sense of the word, and waiting. Thus it appears that waiting and concrete capital must both be regarded as independent factors of production. This is only natural, for no modern process of production could be carried on, *as it actually is carried on*, without the aid of previously existing concrete capital, and without waiting being continually supplied during the whole process.

CHAPTER VI

INTEREST IN THE SOCIALIST COMMUNITY

§ 1. *Economic Principles of the Socialist Community.*

By a "Socialist Community" we shall here understand a community created in order to realise the labourer's "right to the whole produce of his labour." The first condition for this is of course that the community should take possession of all the material means of production ; for no one doubts that private ownership of the means of production implies "income without labour," or "income from property," which, according to the Socialist view, is the very negation of the "right to the whole produce of labour." On the other hand, this right involves that the community shall not interfere with private ownership of goods for consumption ; for if consumption, too, is regulated on communistic principles, there remains no such thing as private rights of an economic nature.

The scheme of distribution of such a Socialist community was drawn up by *Robert Owen*, and later, with still greater accuracy, by the German Socialist *Rodbertus*. The principal point in these schemes is the creation of "labour-money." Common labour of a certain standard is to be regarded as "normal," and an hour of such labour is used as a unit of measurement for all labour, skilled labour of different degrees being reduced to normal labour by the aid of certain figures of reduction. But the "normal hour" is more than that; it is the universal measure of value or price. The labourer receives his wage in the form of a certificate of so many hours' work; and the price of every commodity is simply the number of hours which has been required to produce that commodity. It seems then plausible enough that the labourer, in buying commodities for his certificates, must receive the whole produce of his labour, or at least the full equivalent of that produce.

But a closer examination of the matter will show that this conclusion, so frankly drawn by Socialist authors, is very precipitate. Take, for instance, the typical case of two agricultural labourers producing the same crop on soils of different quality. The cost of production is necessarily lower on the better land; but it would be impossible to sell the same product at two different prices. Selling the whole produce at the higher price, the community makes a profit on the cheaper product. This profit must, of course, in some way be distributed among the members of the community. The labourers are not then, as a class, deprived of any part of the whole produce of their labour; but the particular labourer who worked on the better soil will never get the whole produce of his individual labour.

The same applies in all cases where a commodity is produced at different costs of production. The more modern and better equipped workshop, the factory directed with greater business ability, and the iron-work with the more convenient supply of iron-ore and coal, must all work out profits to the community. Thus the "differential principle" remains in full force in a society organised on Socialistic lines. So does the "principle of scarcity." If any natural agent of production is so scarce that it is impossible to satisfy the demand for it gratis, the community is compelled to put a price on it. Evidently the community thereby makes a profit for itself.

All these profits must ultimately be used for the benefit of the labourer. By means of them the community might, for instance, cover such expenses as are now covered by taxes. It might therefore be argued that the whole body of labourers, as identical with the community, would be receiving the whole produce of its labour. Indeed there is nothing in the nature of the profits, as here considered, to prevent the community from consuming every year an equivalent to the labour of that year. We must, therefore, assume that the incomes of the community are spent in full each year, to the advantage of its members. In what follows, we shall, however, prove that a Socialist community administered on such principles would necessarily end the year with a deficit; and we shall then be brought to conclude that, not only the right of the individual, but even the right of the community to the full produce of its labour is a fallacy.

§ 2. *The Necessity of Interest.*

Let us examine the economy of the Socialist community a little more in detail. We begin with the assumption that there is no progress whatever, *i.e.*, we assume production to go on year after year in precisely the same manner and in the same dimensions.

If all labour were of immediate use for the consumer, the total number of normal hours of work in one year would, of course, always correspond exactly with the total value of commodities at the disposal of the community in that year. Under such circumstances the community would evidently be able to meet every demand guaranteed by a certificate of

labour. But things are not so simple. Much preliminary work must be done in this year which is
not of any use to the consumer before the process of
production has reached its end. On the other hand,
many products ripen in this year, and enter with
their whole value on the credit side of the budget of
the Socialist community, though much labour has
been bestowed upon them in previous years. It is
obvious however that, in the state of absolute
equilibrium here supposed, the number of hours of
labour devoted in one year to the benefit of future
years is exactly the same as the number of hours of
labour in previous years from which the present
year has the benefit. For, otherwise, the total stock
of intermediate goods of the community would
inevitably increase or decrease. Consequently the
fact that production takes time would not prevent
the community from consuming every year the
equivalent, counted in normal hours, to the labour
of that year.

There are other complications arising out of the
fact that consumption of durable goods takes time.
When a house is finished, the use that can be
immediately made of it by the consuming community corresponds only to a very small part of the
total labour expended on it. It would seem therefore, at first sight, as if the Socialist community
must always fall short of its liabilities when building
a house or when constructing any durable goods
whatever. This, however, is not so in the case
of the absolute equilibrium which we are now
considering,

Let us suppose all houses to be of the same
description and each to last for 100 years. We
might then assume that, out of 100 houses, one
must be pulled down every year and another
erected in its place. This group of 100 houses
will then remain invariable : it will always include

houses of 100 different ages from one year up to 100. Supposing one house to cost 100,000 normal hours, the service afforded every year will be worth, according to the Socialist principle that labour alone is to be paid for, 1,000 normal hours, and the services of all houses together will be worth 100,000 normal hours, which is therefore the annual income drawn by the community from the 100 houses. But this sum is exactly the same as that which the community has to spend annually on rebuilding. Consequently, the fact that consumption of durable goods takes time, does not prevent the community from enjoying in every year the equivalent, counted in normal hours, of the labour of that year.

To sum up : under absolutely stationary conditions, the community must spend every year a certain amount of labour, in order to keep up that stock of capital which it once possesses. This labour, *plus* that of which the results are immediately consumed, may be regarded as the cost of the total amount of commodities and services annually placed at the disposal of the consumers. This amount of commodities and services can and must be sold at cost price. The right of the community to the whole produce of its own labour is then realised. There is no reason whatever for charging prices above the bare labour cost ; thus no room is left for interest on capital. And the theorist of Socialism might triumphantly declare that it is after all possible to do away with interest.[1]

---

[1] *Rodbertus* has evidently reasoned under the unconscious assumption of such stationary conditions. This seems also to have been the case with several economists who have admitted that interest could be done away with in a Socialist community. *Sidgwick* for instance says (Principles of Political Economy, III., VI., 6 : "In short, all the 'saving' required *could* be done without being paid for, if it were done by the community previous to the division of the produce." A similar concession is made by *Böhm-Bawerk*.

Still, if we have regard to the conditions under which this result has been obtained, we must at once recognise its entirely hypothetical character. We have as a fact assumed that there should be no progress whatever. But progress must take place, and every step forward must cause a deficit in the budget of the Socialist community.

Indeed, economic progress consists in spending, in one year, more labour than would have been required in order to maintain the old stationary state of things. If this labour can be spent wholly on articles of immediate use, the surplus in labour is balanced by a surplus in consumable goods. But, as a rule, progress requires labour to be spent in production processes which will be completed only in some future year, or on durable goods which will repay immediately only a small part of the labour spent on them. Such extra labour being spent for the sake of progress, there is clearly nothing, or at least very little, in the form of consumable goods, to enter in the current year against those expenses. The labourers will hold certificates to an amount exceeding that which can be met by consumable goods at the disposal of the community. And the community will be bankrupt.

It will, of course, be necessary for the Socialist community to cover such a deficit caused by progress. This can be done only in the way of raising the prices of commodities and services so much above their labour cost that the total profit made on them equalises the quantity of labour invested for the sake of progress. It remains to examine how much of those profits should be charged to each product. We have then only to observe that the ultimate reason why prices must be raised is the fact that the community requires more waiting than it can afford to supply for nothing, as it does in the stationary state. Hence it follows that the Socialist community will have to put a price on waiting ; that is to say, demand interest on its capital. The essence of the matter is this : so long as the community already possesses the whole capital that it wishes to use, it can afford to supply waiting for nothing ; but as soon as it enters upon an increase of its capital, fresh waiting is needed, and this cannot be supplied without a sacrifice on the part of the present labourers ; they must, so long as the community goes on increasing its capital, work more than they consume ; and the right to the whole produce of labour cannot be sustained. This is the fundamental point ; the distribution of the sacrifice over the different consumers is only of secondary importance. But we only apply a general economic principle of universal validity when we say that the Socialist community would have to exact one price for one and the same service, waiting. As it could not supply all the waiting required for nothing, waiting would necessarily command a real positive price, which would enter into the cost of production of the various commodities. Now interest is, by definition, the price of waiting. Hence we arrive at the final conclusion that interest is necessary in a progressive Socialistic community.

It remains to examine how far progress itself must be regarded as necessary. It should be remembered, then, that the measure of progress, in the sense in which the word is taken here, is the growth of capital. The growth of population is the first circumstance compelling the community to increase its capital. Obviously capital must increase in at least the same rate as population, if retrogression is not to take place. Next we have to take account of the necessity, *which must be specially urgent in a Socialist community*, of raising the standard of living among the labourers. A simple equal division of all incomes of the present world would not mean any considerable step forward to the labouring class. The social problem can be solved only by greatly and speedily increasing the total production of the community. Capital, the tool of production, must of course increase at least in the same ratio. Finally, the Socialist community would necessarily have to introduce technical improvements and apply new methods provided by the progress of science, unless it should decide for ever to keep its production at a lower standard of efficiency than would have been reached by a society organised on the present lines.

These considerations show that progress is nothing short of a categorical imperative which the community must obey, irrespective of the forms it chooses to give its economic organisation. Supposing a Socialist community started with the present capital of the world, it would very soon find it absolutely inadequate for its needs. It is hardly conceivable that such a community would be content with a slower growth of capital than the present. Indeed everything makes for the assumption that it would need a much more rapid increase. Let us suppose the community to increase its capital every year 1 per cent. on account of the growth of population, and $1\frac{1}{2}$ per cent. on account of real progress. This is probably not more than what is very often done by our present society. This $2\frac{1}{2}$ per cent. represents a certain quantity of labour which can be paid for only by raising a corresponding sum in the form of interest on the capital of the society. Hence it follows that the Socialist community under the given circumstances would have to charge interest at $2\frac{1}{2}$ per cent. ; this interest being counted as a part of the cost of production, and therefore of the selling price of every commodity.[1]

[1] *Blissard* has, in his " Ethics of Usury and Interest " (pp. 74-75), pointed out some reasons for believing that the members

It is possible that the establishment of the Socialist community would mean a somewhat lower rate of interest than that prevailing in the present society. But it is quite certain that the difference would be very insignificant, and the advantage of this lower rate to the working class is certainly not so great that it is worth while to revolutionise the whole system of social economics. Socialists might claim a higher productive efficiency for their scheme of social organisation ; it is then their duty to bring forward reasonable grounds for such a claim. But they should no longer try to escape this duty by representing interest as the essential evil from which the present society suffers, and pointing to their system as the only remedy from it.

What has just been said of interest under Socialism has no immediate application to the present society. For we are not now bound to that peculiar principle characteristic of the Socialist community, that the total interest income of a year must be equal to the increase of capital in that year. Still it cannot be doubted that the rate of progress, *i.e.* the proportion which the increase of capital bears to the capital already accumulated, has the most important influence on the rate of interest in the world as it is. We spend every year a great amount of productive capacity in adding to the stock already existing, new houses, railways, waterworks, etc., the use of which is, for the most part, reserved for the benefit of the future. We cannot expect to do this without feeling it a sacrifice. The complaint against interest is after all only a complaint that the great advantages of rapid progress cannot be had for nothing.

of the Socialist community would not feel inclined to make such a sacrifice for the sake of progress. The social revolution would then result in stagnation or—in the case of a rapid growth of population—even in retrogression.

CHAPTER VII

SOME PRACTICAL CONCLUSIONS

§ 1. *Interest and Usury.*

TAKING account only of such forces as must be at work under an ideal system of prices, where the cost principle is strictly enforced, we have arrived at the result that, whatever the organisation of society, Waiting necessarily commands a price. This "social value" of waiting is *interest*. Every higher price that might be obtained under the present imperfect system of price-making is *usury*. Of course, waiting is, as we have seen, supplied under very different conditions, and there are accordingly several different rates of interest. The contract "interest" very often includes payment for a certain risk. Still, for every special form of loan, where the circumstances are not of an extraordinary character, there will be a market which fixes the price. The more this market approaches the ideal conditions of the Cost-principle, the more just will be the price. Usury is that surplus price which the lender is able to exact because of the defective organisation of the market, or where the circumstances, particularly the risks, are of such an extraordinary character that no market could possibly exist.

Thus usury is only one variety of that more general form of robbery which consists in taking advantage of the defects of the organisation of the market. And it is not in our days the most important. Indeed, the employer who takes advantage of the misery, the isolation, and the ignorance of his labourers, inflicts upon the present society a more fatal injury than the ordinary usurer who draws his profits from a similar weakness of the borrower. The general condemnation of usury, as compared with the indifference in regard to, or even approval of, the analogous action of the employer, is a striking instance of how moral views are a product of historical evolution.

Having once acquired a clear conception of the nature of usury, we shall have no difficulty in laying down the general lines of a rational policy against this evil. The main problem is how to secure for every legitimate loan that rate of interest which would have been agreed upon, with due regard to all circumstances, under an ideal organisation of the market. Hence it follows immediately that the chief remedy lies in the *organisation of credit*, with the purpose of *securing to everybody the credit he is worth*. This involves not only the creating of organisations, co-operative or otherwise, to provide loans for the small farmer, the artisan, etc., but also the spread of such elementary business-knowledge as will prevent the borrower from entering upon a contract of which he does not quite realise the bearing, and will enable him in some degree to understand the conditions of the market. The fruitfulness of this policy has been established beyond all doubt through the practical experience of most modern countries. As soon as credit becomes, in a broader sense, well organised, we hear nothing more of usurious rates being exacted where a reasonable security is offered, whereas in the Middle Ages exorbitant rates were very often paid on real property.

Thus the centre of gravity of every policy against usury lies in administrative action. There are, however, a good many loans of such a character that they should be altogether prohibited. When the borrower enters upon a contract which he has no reasonable hope of fulfilling, he is clearly guilty of frivolity, and in the interest of public morality he should be punished. It is, therefore, in such cases, rather the action of the borrower, than that of the lender, which should be made a criminal offence. It seems more sensible too to prosecute the borrower, if the intention is to prohibit exorbitant rates of interest. For, according to the principle of demand and supply, the price will fall when demand is restrained, but rise when the supply is restrained. Some thousand years of practical experience have proved that the prosecution of the money lender only results in an extra, and usually a very considerable charge being made, in order to cover the risk of breaking the law.

§ 2. *Interest and Social Distribution.*

In our times, the problem of usury has lost its former predominance, and the theory of interest derives most of its importance from the circumstance that a central position has been attributed to interest in the great modern struggle as to the justice of social distribution. The whole dispute on this point will evidently gain very much in definiteness and simplicity once it is recognised that interest is a price necessary even under an ideal system of prices. A good many well-intentioned persons who have devoted their lives to the solution of the social question have wasted their energy in semi-scientific attempts to prove its wrongfulness. If once this question were thoroughly cleared up, the same energetic criticism might be directed towards the

really weak points in the present scheme of distribution, with immense advantage to social progress.

Much of the antagonism to interest is in reality a
disapproval, not of interest as a form of income, but
of that distribution of property which makes so great
a part of the interest income of the community flow
into the pockets of some few privileged individuals.
That an individual is able to draw from the community an income sufficient to lead a life of comfort
and even of luxury, without devoting to the community in return any personal labour of his own,
will always be regarded as a fundamental im-
morality.[1] But this view involves primarily a
condemnation of such institutions as make it possible
for a person to come into great wealth which he has
not earned, or has earned too easily, or without
corresponding efforts of social usefulness. Social
reformers therefore will first have to direct their
action against the laws of inheritance and the
"unearned increment" of the rent of land, these
being the two principal opportunities for men
coming into wealth created by other persons or
by the community; second, against all forms of
monopoly, natural and artificial, facilitating the
acquiring of large fortunes. To complain of the
inevitable fact that large interest goes with large
capital is senseless ; to attack the very roots of
the unequal distribution of property is at least
intelligible.

Profits are in ordinary discussions very often
confounded with interest, and much of what is
urged against the " Capitalist " is in reality intended
to be urged against the Employer, the Merchant, or
the Speculator. It is probable even that many
people find the distinction between interest and

---

[1] *Ruskin* tells us that there are only two faults of real consequence,—Idleness and Cruelty.—" Sesame and Lilies," Preface,
p. xiv.

profits a purely scientific matter. But it is not so ; it is a distinction of the greatest practical importance. As soon as we have separated the idea of pure interest from "gross profits," the whole problem of profits will at once resolve itself into its elementary parts. We shall find that the policy to be adopted is different for every special kind of profits. First, as regards interest, our investigations make it clear that the rate cannot be lowered by deliberate action of the community. Second, "profits" include a good deal of monopoly rent, the regulation of which naturally lies very much in the hands of the community. For the chief object of good economic policy is, as we have seen, to realise the Cost-principle, and this includes the abolition of all monopolies in virtue of which prices are raised above the cost of production. A third element of profits, and indeed that which corresponds most accurately to the meaning of the word, is the reward of business ability. There can be no doubt that this reward is at the present time very often too high. The experience of the Co-operative Societies and of the working class Limited Companies shows that directors of enterprise can be had at a much lower price. And at the same time it shows how to bring about this end : we have to select the directors from a wider field than has hitherto been the case, and thus increase the supply of business ability. Thus we see how essentially different are the causes which govern the various forms of profit. We can hardly wonder, then, that an almost desperate confusion should result from throwing interest together with so many heterogeneous kinds of income, and trying to discuss them all under the chief title of "profits."

A few words may be added to meet a common objection against interest. It is all very well, some people tell us, that interest should be paid for the capital really required to carry on industry. But in actual life the community has to pay interest on a much larger capital, because the present value of so many industrial enterprises exceeds the capital originally invested. This artificial demand for capital, it is argued, must raise the rate much above what is necessary, the necessary rate being perhaps very small or even nil.

The answer to this objection is very simple. Let us suppose a railway company to have invested originally ten millions in the business, and the shares of the company to have risen subsequently 50 per cent. above par. Suppose that all shares have passed into new hands at the price of 150 per cent., it is evident that this railway requires the use of an extra capital of five millions over and above the original cost. Thus the demand for waiting is artificially increased. But, on the other hand, the supply of waiting, or at least the capacity for such supply, has increased just as much. For the original shareholders have gained five millions, which they can now invest in other enterprises. Supposing they do so, the fact that interest has to be paid on a fictitious capital of five millions can have no influence on the capital market or on the rate of interest. It is only where the original holders consume the surplus value of their shares, or a part of it, that interest will have a tendency to rise. The objection is therefore valid only as against the professional speculator who actually lives on the advance of quotations on the Stock Exchange. It is, however, not probable that enough capital is consumed in this way to appreciably influence the rate of interest.

A similar case is where a new monopoly is created by law. The fact that this monopoly will pass in the market as capital, though it is not real capital, can in itself have no influence on the rate of interest. Neither has the continual creation of fresh " capital " by the "unearned increment" of land values any direct influence on the rate. Such alterations of the distribution of income may, however, diminish the desire of saving in the classes on which the new monopolies lay perhaps a new burden.

The social problem is often looked upon as a case of "Capital versus Labour." We are told that the reason why Labour gets so little is that Capital takes so much, or, even in so many words, that abolition of interest would in the main solve the problem. This view is entirely wrong. In the first place, interest *cannot* be done away with. In the second place, an equal distribution of the present interest-income of the community, though it would of course be an advantage to the labourer, would not essentially alter his standard of life. Calculations on this point which confine themselves to England are misleading, for that country draws a very large sum of interest from abroad, and this would disappear if interest were abolished by a general social revolution. But, considering the whole civilised world, it must be said that an equal distribution of the total present interest-income would raise wages only by a fractional part of what they now are.

Hence the conception that the social problem is essentially a question of division of income between Capital and Labour, is seen to be erroneous. Even an equal distribution of *all* income would probably not bring the whole society up to the standard of the lower middle-class. The social problem is, therefore, essentially a problem of greater production. The fundamental fact to start from is that we do not to-day produce enough to provide every one with a decent living. It follows from this that we must produce more. Progress is largely a rise of productive efficiency.

It is generally believed that what Labour gains is necessarily a loss to Capital. This is surely a fallacy.

There are even some reasons for assuming the contrary to be the case.   When wages rise, there is a
tendency for interest to rise too.

First, in so far as a considerable rise of wages
requires that the whole volume of production should
be enlarged, it means at least a proportional increase
in the demand for the use of capital.

Second, the nature of the consumption of the
working-classes makes it often necessary to use
comparatively more machine labour than would
be required for the corresponding consumption of
the rich, for this latter is to a large extent a consumption of personal services, such as those of
domestic servants, artists, and other professional
persons ; whereas the working classes mostly consume products of factory industry.

Third, the increasing productivity of society is to
a large extent a direct result of the substitution of
durable instruments of production for labour.   Inasmuch, therefore, as higher wages require such an
increase of productivity, they also tend to augment
the demand for capital.   To a certain extent the
higher productivity is due to more efficient labour ;
but the higher efficiency of the working man shows
itself precisely in the capacity for handling complicated and expensive machinery.   It should also be
remembered here that higher wages directly encourage the substitution of machine labour for hand
labour.

Thus a rise of wages is seen to have a strong
tendency towards raising the demand for the use of
capital.   It is probable too that a rise of wages
would restrain the supply of waiting.   For if the
labourer really is to raise his standard of life, he
cannot save any considerable part of the increase in
his wages.   The increased production therefore is
not accompanied by a proportional increase in the
capacity for saving.

Hence we must conclude that a rise of wages.is very likely to call forth a *rise* and not a *fall* of the rate of interest. This conclusion, one may hope, is calculated to contradict the common dogmatic view, and definitely relieve the world of an old and barren controversy.

INDEX TO AUTHORS